Sorry I Haven't Texted You Back

a collection of poems by

Alicia Cook

Andrews McMeel
PUBLISHING®

For those who often feel
alone in their head.
This is your reminder:
you aren't.

*Written between July 2018
and February 2020*

Dedicated
to my sister.

This book contains
sensitive material relating to:

Mental Health, Illness
Guns and Other Weapons, Violence
Suicide
Drugs and Alcohol
Natural Disaster
Death
Sex
Trauma

and possibly more that can be triggering to survivors.

Please take care of yourself
during,
after,
ALWAYS

Hi. Sorry I haven't texted you back. ~~I've been anxious and depressed.~~ I haven't had time to catch my breath, you know how life gets. ~~I am so drained I can't even collect the energy for the most menial of tasks, like texting you back or washing the one dish in the sink.~~ The weather has been beautiful, right? ~~Yesterday I fought off a panic attack while I was driving. I had to pull over because my vision was blurred. I focused on how blue the sky was. I haven't washed my hair in three days. I just want to sleep all the time, but if I told you, you would want to uncover a reason behind all of this, and there is no tangible reason you would accept as valid.~~ How are you? I hope well. Let's get dinner soon!

Written by *Alicia Cook*
Illustrated by *Katie Curcio*

Also by Alicia Cook

Stuff I've Been Feeling Lately

I Hope My Voice Doesn't Skip

"Life goes on,
days get brighter."

– Mac Miller

SIDE A

The Poems.

Track One

I tell you I feel tired
and you say,
"But you slept for twelve hours,"
and I knew you didn't get it.

I tell you maybe I need Vitamin D
and you crack a joke about your dick;
and I knew you didn't get it.

You tell me I have
"nothing to be sad about."
I agree and you meet me with a shrug;
and I knew you didn't get it.

I tell you the noise and the crowd are
getting to me and you say, "I told you
that you didn't have to come;"
and I knew you didn't get it.

I tell you my temples feel heavy
and you say, "Take Advil;"
and I knew you didn't get it.

You suggest maybe another shower,
or makeup,
or a run will lift my spirits;
and I knew you didn't get it.

I tell you, and tell you,
and tell you and you never get it.
Don't worry.
It's not your fault . . .

I get it.

Currently listening to:
"Different Kind of Tears" by Sully Erna

3

Track Two

No one knows how much she cried last Wednesday. Because she still hit her marks. She got out of bed, though she didn't fix the covers. She showered but forgot to rinse out the conditioner. She put on clean clothes, though they were a bit wrinkled.

There were no runs in her tights, no mascara clumps by her eyes. She was only five minutes late, which is considered "on time" when you're running on four hours of sleep and Seasonal Depression. She didn't engage in conversation but greeted everyone with a smile. She went home without an appetite but still cooked dinner. She had sex but didn't finish.

No one knows how much she cried last Wednesday because she was quiet about it, and to some, pain is only noticed when it is public, and loud, and obvious. No one knows how much she cried last Wednesday because Thursday was better and, by then, she didn't want to dwell on yesterday.

Currently listening to:
"You Don't Know How It Feels" by Tom Petty

Track Three

We may sleep together,
but my dreams are my own.

That's always been my problem. I shut
people out. I only let them see me from
certain angles, in certain lighting, at
certain moments. My mother says it's
because I am independent. My therapist
says it's my defense mechanism. My ex
says it's why we broke up. My friends
say they love me anyway.

I say it's because I feel
safest in half measures.

I'll love you—but not completely.
I'll hold your hand—but won't
interlace our fingers.
I'll take pictures—but won't tag you.
I'll miss you—but never enough to ever
question leaving.

Currently listening to:
"What Now" by Rihanna

Track Four

For now, I will say
I wanted to take a picture
of you in the car.
The sun was setting
and there was this tugging on my heart,
telling me I was going to want
to remember this part.

But I knew a photo
wouldn't live up to
what my eyes were living,
so I just stared at you
until the sun disappeared
behind a building.

For now, I will say
when we were walking
around the harbor,
if it weren't for the people
with umbrellas running for cover,
I would have never felt the rain
or heard the thunder.

And if you knew what my mind
was like before,
you'd get what I meant
that gray morning,
when I said you were the only one
who could make me forget
it was pouring.

Currently listening to:
"Flagship" by Jason Isbell

Track Five

I don't tell you that I went to work today in the shirt I slept in last night. I don't tell you that I cried on the couch for no fucking reason.

I don't tell you that I am hungover in the middle of the week. I don't tell you I can't recall the last time my mind didn't hurt.

I don't need to tell you any of this for you to sense that burnout is imminent. You don't need to know the whole story to understand the story.

That is why you are beautiful.

You tell me you are here if I want to talk. You tell me I better sleep tonight because the bags under my eyes are atrocious. You tell me I better eat and take an iron pill.

I don't push back. I sincerely tell you that I am trying. You believe me, and you believe in me. And that's the precarious, precious cycle that keeps me going.

Thank you for not needing the whole story to understand the story.

Currently listening to:
"Most of All" by Brandi Carlile

Track Six

I implore you

crawl out of that grave
before the dust settles
before the grass returns.

Before you get too comfortable
with death, with oblivion.
Before your fingerprints
and footprints are wiped clean.
Before the world
gets used to spinning without you.

You're too priceless
to remain lifeless
in cheap pine.
In a dress you didn't choose.
In caked-on makeup.
You never slept well on your back.

Break your nails.
Scuff your knuckles.
Swallow the ground.
B l o o m.

You belong here on the surface,
with pomegranates and rain and fig
trees, with traffic and lavender and
morning breath.

Not wherever comes next.
Not yet.

Not on a day like this
when
your existence helps others exist.

Currently listening to:
"Reasons Not to Die" by Ryn Weaver

Track Seven

You were warned about me. Cautioned
that my baseline temperament is restless.
That at the slightest, misconstrued touch,
I would explode like acid-covered
confetti, float gently onto you, burn holes
in your skin, blister your heart, corrode
your belief that love is worth the risk.

You were told I've always been like
this—scar tissue and armor.

All because someone else dripped their
poison onto me, and my lonesome
wounds were looking for company
before they healed. Heartache is just
another contagious disease.

Currently listening to:
"Wandering Child" by Wild Rivers

Track Eight

I hold my breath; this is the test.
I can't exhale until you go to voicemail.
I let it ring through,
let my anxiety brew.
You are not good for my health.
I am getting mad at myself.

For still wanting to answer,
for still wanting an answer.
For ignoring the disparities,
for feigning clarity.

It was October seventeenth,
tree leaves more orange than green,
your eyes still just as blue.
Resurrecting what we grieved,
haunted by the hues.

There's nothing left to say,
though 1,000 words remain.
You were too selfish to be patient,
and I was too sad to stay.
We both know this was never okay.

Re-stitching old patterns,
rehashing old fights.
Replaying the times
the love felt right.

Those moments are
few and far between.
By that I mean, for every slow song,
there were five bloodcurdling screams.

The first year, I cried every night.
Year two, I stopped
romanticizing the bruise.
By year three I was free,
and that's when my phone rang.
It was like you knew
that I was finally okay.

It was October seventeenth.
I set the scene,
STARRING YOU AND ME!
Then I douse that scene in gasoline.

Currently listening to:
"Mercury in Retrograde" by Sturgill Simpson

Track Nine

We were too busy trying to survive the earthquake to even contemplate what it meant that our world had been split open.

We were too busy chasing survival that we didn't even consider that the acts of surviving and restoring would hurt too.

We were too busy crying in frigid tombs, not worrying about unmade beds, dirty dishes, or keeping a calendar, that we forgot that normalcy gives off warmth.

We were too busy picking up broken glass that we normalized our trauma, started to liken the gathering of shards to collecting shells along the shore, or inspecting snowflakes; each one unique in its sharpness, in its deadliness.

We were too busy obsessing over how something we wouldn't ask for in one million years could show up unannounced and dictate our lives in a such a way, that our memories became distorted, or amplified, or went missing altogether.

We were too busy drawing lines in the sand and biting tongues and preparing for war, that we forgot that once upon a time there was a peace.

Currently listening to:
"Home" by Ingrid Michaelson

Track Ten

Your pupils dilated
when I walked in the room
and I knew I had you.

I used to wonder what it'd be like
to kiss you at midnight.
Now we share the same
bar of soap in the shower
and I wake up in love with you.
I kiss your face
where a strip of sunlight
touches your cheek every morning.

It's as though you're not just the love of
my life, but the love of all my lifetimes.
Like we've been here before,
like we'll be here again.

And again. And again.
Looping in a way
that doesn't make me dizzy.

Currently listening to:
"Is That Alright?" by Lady Gaga

Track Eleven

Sometimes I feel like I only feel anything
when something is going wrong;
that I only drive this far down the
turnpike when I am losing my mind.

My tires mold to the familiar roads back
to my old life where muscle memory
replaces the need for GPS; where you
can't turn left so things have to go right;
where there exist people who can
reintroduce me to myself.
I trust that those I trust with my life can
help bring me back to life.

Because no one new
knew me at my best.
My old friends were there
before the detonator blew.
They hold me, wrap me in
time-traveling truths,
and there is comfort.

Currently listening to:
"Count on Me" by Bruno Mars

Track Twelve

We've started to hold our breath
in a world of breathable air.
Hands as raw as Lady Macbeth;
when love is war, all is not fair.

When you said
you loved me in red,
I wish you had said
that you loved me instead.

We've confused passion and pain,
turned each other into liars.
We have become colliding trains;
no survivors, no survivors.

Currently listening to:
"Song About You" by Mike Posner

Track Thirteen

I brush my teeth
and overthink
over the sink.
There are layers to loving me
and most of them aren't pretty.

My reflection doesn't compute.
I don't look like a girl
who has nothing to lose
but I feel like one—I've come undone.

It's the nature of my beast;
I care the most or I care the least,
never ever in between.

Fuzzy pictures to match my life,
could never get the focus right.
Caught up in moving on or staying put;
looking forward, stealing a second look.

So the story always goes,
I'm your soulmate or your foe,
writer's blocked or on a roll.

My heart isn't conditioned
to listen
to anything but its own beat.
There are layers to loving me;
but to the naked eye, I
am just here brushing my teeth.

Currently listening to:
"clementine" by Halsey

Track Fourteen

The spring we met,
I was more wilt than bloom.
I'm not saying you saved me,
but your face and eyes and laugh
made me look back long enough to
think twice.

My second chance was quiet;
only I heard it, but you were there
when it happened and that's enough.

How lucky I am
to have stayed long enough
to play with the hair
at the nape of your neck.

To learn the reasons
behind your nail biting
and the scar between your eyebrows.

To feel you twitch
and to have our bare feet
touch in our sleep.

To eat shrimp tacos with you
in front of the television.

I would have missed out on so much.
I would have missed out on the person
I became since knowing you.

Currently listening to:
"I'm With You" by Vance Joy

Track Fifteen

My throat's collecting dust;
I haven't sung in months.
So overwhelmed by what I need to do
that my to-do list goes untouched.

I can't hold this pose forever.
My legs are starting to tremor.
It's so damn hard to measure up.

I have scrapes on these knees from
praying too hard,
and scrapes on my heart from
staying too long.

Oh, I'm broken,
even dreams take their toll and
I need to regain focus.
Goals come with strings,
and when I say I'm tired
you don't get what I mean.

I'm feeling the worst pain.
Just trying to save face.
Sitting in therapy wondering why
I keep getting in my own way.

I am a mosaicked woman,
making choices a bit crooked.
Doing things I really shouldn't do.

I have aches in my brain from
wondering too hard,
and aches in my legs from
wandering too far.

I'm only human,
running on fumes and
sobbing at red lights.

I'm only human,
paying my dues and
losing my might.

I'm only human,
lying to myself
saying I'm all right.

Currently listening to:
"2 Places" by Tori Kelly

Track Sixteen

You don't know it, but someone you passed in the mall was buying clothes for a funeral.

Someone sitting in the hospital waiting room as you welcomed a life, was mentally preparing to say goodbye to a life.

Someone who ordered coffee in front of you felt like their world stopped turning, but still had to get up with their alarm clock.

Someone next to you in traffic was missing their mother, or father, or sibling, or kid, or pet.

Someone you saw in the park was holding hands with a child who was just introduced to death at an age when they can't grasp the concept of "gone for good." So, they secretly figured they'd ask Santa for them back come Christmas.

Someone on the train cried themselves to sleep or was too devastated to sleep.

Someone you work with woke up to a buzzing phone and the worst news of their life and still showed up seven minutes before you did.

Odds are, you nudged shoulders on a busy street with a broken human today, and you didn't even know it. Practice empathy.

Practice kindness. Always.

Currently listening to:
"Masterpiece" by Pistol Annies

Track Seventeen

You're not good today.

The light hurts your eyes and you left
the house without washing your face so
it's 2:00 p.m. and you are still wiping
away crust from the corners of your
eyes.

You're not good today.

The weather is affecting your mood and
you are crying too easily at
commercials, so you put on something
you've seen a trillion times.

You're not good today.

You've been tired since you woke up
but your mind won't quiet down
enough to rest, so you light a candle at
3:18 a.m. and decide you'll call your
parents later on in the morning.

You're not good today,
and you're good with that.

You understand your mind and your
body; you know even though you're
down, you're not down for the count.
You breathe in and out. You will not let
today obstruct the potential in
tomorrow.

Currently listening to:
"Shake It Out" by Florence + The Machine

Track Eighteen

They ask me again
why I dropped the rose on your coffin
but kept the stem.

Sometimes
time doesn't hold up
its end of the bargain,
and water doesn't
regrow the gardens.
Sometimes time,
try as it might,
can't keep its word
and doesn't heal you
from what occurred.

When they ask me
how long you've been dead,
you die in my head all over again.

Currently listening to:
"Dancing in the Sky" by Dani and Lizzy

Track Nineteen

For a long time, I couldn't shake a snow globe without being reminded of your indiscretions.

The day my eyes watched you leave, my body stayed on the stoop and the first snow of the year started. I remember thinking, *How fucking poetic.*

It never occurred to me that I could stay warm in my skin after what we weathered.

The gusts from the storms of our saga blew scraps of you into my face. You were in photos, in text messages, in strangers, in song lyrics, in certain smells, in clothes of mine I knew you loved.

There's stability in the aftermath of instability. There's beauty in hard transitions.

Though it may seem magical and
swift from the outside, any
transformation can be gruesome deep
inside the chrysalis.

The butterfly would confess this to us if
we understood her language.

By the time the first snow of another
year began to fall without you, and my
street quietly transformed into
something else as I slept, I was okay. I
had become someone different inside of
my familiar skin, and I was okay.

This is still a love poem
even if I don't love you anymore.

Currently listening to:
"It Wasn't Easy to Be Happy for You" by The Lumineers

Track Twenty

I've sort of gotten used to seeing
my family be a family without me on
the internet.

My own absence barely fazes me;
because the less I post, the more I reveal
and the less I scroll, the better I feel.

I am worried about the state of art.

       IT'S
            ALL TOO
                       STATE OF
                       THE ART.

It's surface level,
nothing to it:
elevator music.

Currently listening to:
"In Another Time" by Disturbed

Track Twenty-One

As we kiss in the car, I find myself
purposely inhaling your breaths deep
into my lungs. I know I need to take in as
much of you as I can.

"Let's go watch the sunset," you suggest,
putting the car in gear.

"Are we going to make it?" I ask,
peering out the window as the
sun dips behind the trees.

"Yeah. Definitely," you answer.

I let you go on believing that I am asking
about the sunset.

Currently listening to:
"Consequences" by Camila Cabello

Track Twenty-Two

Nervous, uncertain,
rambling, but wordless;
the pain, it immersed us.

You got the broom and swept up the
glass and broken trust.
Found needles from the cedar from our
last happy Christmas.

The hatchets we planted
in the dead of winter
bloomed in June.

That's the thing about civil wars,
they're always more personal.
That's the thing about closed doors,
they're always more confessional.
That's the thing about hearts like yours,
they're just so damn merciful.

Currently listening to:
"Better Man" by Little Big Town

Track Twenty-Three

The creatures from my deep won't stay
submerged forever.

They will surface and sing or scream.
They will touch sunlight and bask or
burn.

And I will have no control
over any of this.

It happens suddenly.
I could be fine for days, weeks, months.

Until I am not.

Reminiscences and tears
are bees that sting.
Suddenly. Quickly.
Maybe not even on purpose.
First instinct is to swat,
but I know they'll be extinct one day
and I can't yet imagine a world where
these memories don't sporadically
buzz through my bramble brain.

I brush up against a memory,
ever so briefly, accidentally.
And the wound opens.

Today, I took a sip of cucumber water
but tasted my past and was reminded
that you don't have to deliberately
pick at a scab for it to bleed.

Currently listening to:
"Not Today" by Alessia Cara

Track Twenty-Four

Don't know where I buried the bones.
It takes a village, but I prefer to be alone.
How do I silence my mind
like I silence my phone?
Heavy lies this crown;
I want to be dethroned.

They say the train runs best on the track,
but what if it's going in the wrong
direction?

I got a liar in my ear making me
question if I would drown, but turns
out, I can breathe underwater.

Looking up
from this downward spiral.
Hard to ride
the waves when they're tidal.
I lose my grip
trying to hold on the longest.
I came here to be honest,
not the strongest.

Fuck the pedestal,
I'm doing the best that I can.
Fuck your pedestal,
because I never said I was
who you think I am.

Currently listening to:
"Overtime" by Big Sean

Track Twenty-five

There is still snow on the ground and you can't, for the life of you, recall the last time you saw snow this far along in the spring. But soon, the time will come for dodging dripping air conditioners that hang from windows that will never know central air. The cash-only ice cream parlor will open for the season in a few short weeks. The warmth is coming even though all you can feel is cold right now. The ice you nearly slipped on in the parking lot this morning is nothing but a puddle come afternoon and will freeze over again once the sun goes to sleep. All of these small things are signs that air shifting and blooming daffodils and songbirds will be here soon.

Currently listening to:
"I Can See Clearly Now" by Johnny Nash

Track Twenty-Six

I'm in my own head a lot.

Last night you caught me staring at the wall for far too long. Sometimes, I can't sleep for days, which affects you when it's 2:47 a.m. and I try to have a conversation with you; because that is when the fog lifts and I am awake.

I forget to call you when I get home and you get frustrated when I abandon my shoes in the middle of the room or don't charge my phone (it's on 8% right now, so I need to make this quick).

I don't make beds or fold clothes—I'll wear your socks and boxers to bed. You sigh really hard each time I don't use a coaster, but that won't condition me to care about condensation.

All of this is difficult.
I know.

I am a hard person to love. None of this makes me eccentric or an enigma or artistic.

It makes me a
neurotic pain in the ass.

Sparks did not fly when you met me,
those were warning flares,
d i s t r e s s signals.

Currently listening to:
"when the party's over" by Billie Eilish

33

Track Twenty-Seven

They kissed *goodbye* instead of *see you tomorrow.*

To this day, they wonder if the other detected the subtle differences. Like how they held one another a bit longer, a bit tighter. How they walked away slowly, turning around to ensure that the other's smiling face was burned into their memory. They wonder if the other noticed how the "I love you" that left their lips was their most honest declaration, said slowly and deliberately, because they knew they could never say it again.

Did they hear the slight break in voice? They wonder if the other felt them press close, ear-to-chest, just to feel the heartbeat through the other's shirt before it broke, healed, and began beating for someone else. They wonder if the other saw how they sat in the car, long after firing up the engine, begging their heart to stop dragging its feet and get in the shotgun seat so they could drive away.

They wonder if the other knows that not everyone who *has* to leave, *wants* to leave.

Currently listening to:
"Doesn't Just Go" by Carly Moffa

Track Twenty-Eight

Loaded livers and statements
tonight in this basement bar.
Your fingers are too far away.

Trading repartee
between red wine sips.
I catch you staring
at my lips.
Then you joke about
the age difference.

But I have caught up

in decades
   and mindsets
      and regrets.

In lost games
   and upsets
      and life tests.

You say that you should go,
but you don't leave your seat.
We brace for our impact
and the flames it will bring.

You and me,
lost and found,
lost and foundering.

Currently listening to:
"If I Told You" by Darius Rucker

Track Twenty-Nine

To the untrained eye, these coping mechanisms often look a lot like self-destruction.

The binge drinking. The binge sleeping. The insomnia. The dust on the ceiling fans, the ring around the tub. The wallowing. The nonstop working. The procrastinating. The canceling therapy last minute so they still take your co-pay. The toothpaste spit on the mirror. The phone that hasn't been charged. The *Are you still watching 'The Office?'* prompts. The drives where you can't remember taking the turns but still wind up at your destination. The writer's block. The missed calls and *The mailbox you wish to reach is full* dismissals. The unwashed hair, the un-run dishwasher. The oil splatter that has made itself comfortable on the stove.

It's all needed. Maybe to destroy yourself just enough so your current existence can no longer be sustained. This way, there will be no other choice but to rebuild, to come back as the person you've earned the right to become.

Currently listening to:
"Maybe It's Time" by Bradley Cooper

Track Thirty

When you meet a writer,
they won't write about you.

You'll kiss and have sex and smile,
and they won't write about you.

You'll fall in love,
befriend each other's friends,
and they won't write about you.

You'll binge-watch shows,
learn how they take their coffee,
and they won't write about you.

You might be together one year,
five years, a decade; dancing together
at weddings and consoling one
another at funerals, and they won't
write about you.

Then it will   fall
                                    apart.

You will leave or they will leave, or
you'll both stay and start sleeping back-
to-back, because staying is easier than
leaving, and *that* is when they will write
about you.

Currently listening to:
"Happy" by Julia Michaels

Track Thirty-One

Sunglasses are dark,
car's in park—just idling.
My numbness is frightening.

Overthinking again,
biting the inside of my mouth,
picking at my cuticles.

In need of a friend;
lonely living in a world
addicted to pharmaceuticals.

Currently listening to:
"The Season / Carry Me" by Anderson .Paak

Track Thirty-Two

You never appreciated my presence, but you feel my absence in your joints and arteries. In the mornings you wake, eyelids dusted with frost because you were only dreaming of my warmth. Your fantasies were too busy wondering, your hands were too busy reaching in wrong directions to hold onto what mattered. Until what mattered decided you didn't matter. Until what mattered left with a new number and lover and priorities. You never loved me, but your heart broke just the same the day I stopped loving you and began to love myself.

Currently listening to:
"Minute" by Caitlin Mahoney

Track Thirty-Three

The Devil's making lemonade
out of my dilemmas.
I'm not antisocial—
but I don't speak venom.
It's a slippery slope,
to deny it or cope.
Won't know 'til I hit water
if I will sink or float.

The more you console me,
the lonelier I get.
I know you can't handle
the loose threads in my head.
I must be something to see,
weeping under the willow tree,
trying to get out the knots
in the necklace you gave me.

I leave with the ease
of a traveling, tented show.
I can't see your face,
and your voice I won't recall.
Because the dead keep breathing
only when you let them talk.

But please hold off on the dispatch,
I'm on the mend.
I'll keep my hope in a bottle
so it won't sail off again.

Currently listening to:
"Heroes and Songs" by Brandi Carlile

Track Thirty-Four

You'll think my idiosyncrasies are sexy
until you see them barefaced, no
makeup.

But I AM RUNNING OUT OF
METAPHORS TO MAKE HOW
SHITTY I FEEL more digestible,
quotable, poetic.

My overthinking is only romantic when
it is described as a wanderlust mind that
spans galaxies; not when I call it what it
is, *obsessive and intrusive.*

My tense and achy muscles only hold
appeal when they arrive alongside a
photo of my body.

My tears remain drinkable when the
bloodshot lines burning my eyes match
the stellar patterns of Orion.

Healing is only healing when it's linear and universal, blended with stardust and glitter; not when it's inconsistent and personal, mixed with grit and couches.

Reality disturbs some of the same people who plead for authenticity.

When will they realize they are one and the same?

They still try though, to take the literal out of context. To make pain more digestible, quotable, poetic.

Pretty, even.
It's none of those things.

Currently listening to:
"Goddess" by Banks

Track Thirty-Five

Most of what enters my head arrives
uninvited. Chaos swarms the perimeter
of my calm. There are storm patterns
lined in my palms.

Lightning may not strike the same place
twice but my cyclonic thoughts ravage
again and again.

(Inevitability has a noise. Only I hear the
hum.)

It's not creative or clean.
        It's manic and messy.
It's not slow and controlled.
        It's sudden and out of my hands.

Like waking up with a runny nose
because someone else left the window
open on the coldest night of the year.

Currently listening to:
"What We Stay Alive For" by Sleep On It

Track Thirty-Six

The truth has a tendency
to drip out a little at a time,
like water from a loose faucet
in the middle of the night.

Life can be tough
when you've never done well
with ticking clocks
or fights on city blocks
(or ultimatums or small talk).

The cough syrup at the pharmacy
reminds me of the energy thing
you used to drink when we were young.
When we took those rides
to nowhere with the radio up.
We all miss who we were back then.
We're all scared of who we'll become,
when all is said and done.

Currently listening to:
"Now I'm In It" by Haim

Track Thirty-Seven

Lately I have been dreaming of another realm outside of this dystopia where "umpteenth" is an actual number and "someday" is a day of the week and "soon" and "eventually" are realistic measurements of time.

A world where wishes can be granted by weeds and stars and flickering candles. A world where you can have the impossible, like time machines for second chances or the hollow bones of a bird to fly away from whatever has hurt you.

I am drained from breathing here, in a world with last words and final hugs, where we have to worry about clocks running out and saying goodbye to people we know we can't live without but will have to one day. It is hard to live in this world of inevitabilities.

Then, the first frost of the season dances up my windows, or the red-winged blackbird flutters back to its branch where leaves have also returned, or the summer sun blazes deep into the evening hours, or the smell from a wood-burning fireplace mixes with the air, and I am no longer weary.

During these soft transitions, when you can taste the faint hint of a rainbow, what truly matters in life rises above all the insignificance to its rightful place on the surface, and what should have always mattered the most becomes what matters most once again.

Currently listening to:
"Rainbow" by Kacey Musgraves

Track Thirty-Eight

We kiss and my lipstick
ends up on your coffee lid.
The way your breath touches my ear—
we are alone, everywhere.

You don't know what you do for me—
or to me—
the lightning you course through me.
My feet have found solid ground.
Skies have parted—no dark clouds.
You managed to slow me down just
enough to pause, to breathe,
to turn my life around.

And I hope you are still here
this time next year.

We can wake up to change
and we don't have much say
in what breaks our way,
or how long people stay;

but before I met you my mind
and my heart were at odds all the time.
Then you floated in on a dandelion wish
and ever since knowing you exist,
I just want to sit, count your eyelashes.

And I hope you are still here
this time next year.

I've never been synonymous
with keeping promises,
but this is different.

If you don't,
then I won't
disappear.

And we'll still be here
this time next year.

Currently listening to:
"if we never met" by John K (featuring Kelsea Ballerini)

Track Thirty-Nine

Things too many of us do:

- Mimic the excitement in the room at gender reveals, bridal showers, and our own birthdays.
- Smile when everyone around us is smiling; keep up with social cues.
- Wonder why three hours felt like twelve.
- Wonder why we couldn't sleep.
- Wonder why we couldn't collect the energy to shower, put clothes away, or go to the gas station.
- Blame our period. Blame retrograde. Blame Vitamin D deficiency.
- Lie to our partners. Lie to our parents. Lie every Tuesday and say we were going to the gym, but go to therapy.
- Go home and cry. Go home and be too drained to even charge our phones because pretending we were fine every day has begun to exhaust us.
- Go home and Google "anxiety" and "depression."
- Clear search history.

Currently listening to:
"fake smile" by Ariana Grande

Track Forty

A lot stays buried under
feet that are stationary.
You said being with me *felt heavy*
and my composure cracked
under the weight of that.

I've developed a habit
of lighting matches
then staying in the room,
taking in the fumes, for too long.

I'm not trying to be dramatic,
but these are the facts:
breakdowns are stealthy.
I just want to be healthy
and happy with where I'm at.

Currently listening to:
"Black Water" by Reuben and the Dark

Track Forty-One

Our last hug, you lifted me off the
ground like you wanted to take me with
you, like you didn't want to let me go,
but you left me there.

And yet,
when you placed me back on my feet,
my knees didn't buckle.
I remained standing.
That's how I knew that
plot twists don't always have to feel
like the turning of a knife.
They can feel like the bridge
in your favorite song.
They can feel like daylight on your face.
They can feel like a second chance
at a better life.

Currently listening to:
"I Refuse" by Aaliyah

Track Forty-Two

A month ago, when this was planned, you were excited. Now you are filled with dread because you wanted your friend to cancel and can't articulate why. You catch your reflection and want to cry; not over how you look, but over how you feel inside. That's when you unravel. Agonize over scenarios that will never happen. Overanalyze moments that already played out. Scroll mindlessly through social media when you should be getting dressed. You're supposed to meet your friend at 8:00. It's already 8:15. You lie and text, *on my way*. You splash water on your face. Get your breathing under control. You're not going to be on time, but you will be there. You are going to be late. Again. You are going to blame the traffic, not your anxiety. Again.

Currently listening to:
"The World at Large" by Modest Mouse

Track Forty-Three

Life is a mix of choices and chance.
A cross between best of luck
and best-laid plans.

Sometimes it feels like the cards
I've been dealt
were shuffled by the Devil himself.
I can read his tell.

Adam never needed to learn;
he had Eve up his sleeve.

I don't go to church anymore unless
someone is baptized, married, or dead;
but I still bless myself whenever
I am about to run a red
and keep the palm cross
tucked in my car above my head.

I let men with biblical names drag me
through Hell for the art it creates.
Have you seen my faith?
It seems to have been misplaced
somewhere beyond the saints, and
snakes, and apples, and gardens.

Forgive me, Father, or don't,
I'm not really looking for a pardon.

Currently listening to:
"Walk on Water" by Eminem
(featuring Beyoncé)

Track Forty-Four

So much of me belongs to people who
no longer breathe. It doesn't leave much
for the ones still around me.

Graveyards are for your bones and my
tears, for your name engraved and
supermarket flowers. Graveyards are
for the mourning doves and old
memories and new soil.

I'm usually the only person here,
shooing away the geese.
Why do lines wrap around the corners
of funeral homes, but the cemeteries are
always empty?

Where are the lines?

Where was the line when I could no
longer conjure the sound of your voice?

Where was the line the first time I heard
your laugh come out of someone else's
throat?

Where was the line when they
demolished our favorite restaurant?

Where was the line when your scent left
the pillow or the day I realized I had
seen every single photo of us together
and cried?

Where was the line on your birthday, or
my birthday, or that random

Wednesday when I needed you just
because?

Where are the lines?

The living speak of normal
as if there is such a thing.
Even the mundane is insane
when you are bereaved.
I am starting to believe it's all a game;
that the ones who remain are only here
because we won a round
of musical graves.
We were still breathing
when the music stopped.

A cardinal lands,
the patron bird
of those who have passed.
The lines are gone,
but you,
you are still here.

Currently listening to:
"REMember" by Mac Miller

Track Forty-five

You have your headphones on with no music playing; you just want to pretend you can't hear what they're saying. You've adapted to your own mind. AS IN, even your heavy thoughts seem light. AS IN, your eye hardly twitches anymore. AS IN, you've adjusted to your sleep schedule. AS IN, you don't sleep much at all but found the perfect under-eye concealer.

It's only when you're in a room filled with people not wired in such a way that you realize how close you are to short-circuiting. You are fried. Burned out. Praying for a factory reset you know won't come.

Life tripped you up then challenged you to keep up. Life continued to outpace your strides even after it saw you slumped over, gasping for air. Life kept moving forward even after you began lying to the people around you. AS IN, you didn't say your behavior was directly related to your reluctant metamorphosis. AS IN, you said that you were busy, not broken.

Currently listening to:
"A Patient Year" (live performance) by Chris Rockwell

Track Forty-Six

Biting my loose tongue
listening to Whitney in Houston,
I Wanna Dance with Somebody
who won't leave when the song is done.

I yearned to *Run to You*
when you flew away.
I yearned to *Run to You*
but my flight was delayed.

Will I always fall for the Drifters,
the Rolling Stones, and shape-shifters?
Won't somebody *Stand by Me*
for more than just one picture?

Room Full of Tears,
and all of them mine.
Room Full of Tears,
I needed a sign.

Riding shotgun in a *Fast Car*
with Tracy Chapman and her guitar.
Couldn't choose between the *Crossroads*
so I ran out of gas, never made it far.

Give Me One Reason
to glance in my rearview.
Give Me One Reason
to be near you.

Unobstructed skyline,
I reminisce when I hear Sublime,
about ocean fronts, dollar beers,
and the *Summertime*.

Love was *What I Got*
when I got you.
Indifference was *What I Got*
when we fell through.

Months go by,
trying to see the *Brightside*.
So I run with The Killers
and breathe in high tide.

All the Things I Have Done
weigh on my shoulders,
All the Things I Have Done
brought me my closure.

Sittin' on the Dock of the Bay,
contemplatin' the Otis-way.
Boats bob against weathered posts,
my broken heart still has good days.

I've Been Loving You Too Long
to remember much else.
I've Been Loving You Too Long,
I need to find myself.

Survived all Four Seasons
of your exit with no reasons.
When you miss me, *Tell It to the Rain*.
I found something new to believe in.

Oh, What a Night
it was when I let you go.
Oh, What a Night
it is to go on with the show.

Currently listening to:
"Give Me One Reason" by Tracy Chapman

Track Forty-Seven

I've been using the energy I can muster
to force together apologies and promises
like a child frustrated that the puzzle
pieces don't fit, when they absolutely
look like they should.

I'm sorry I'm so tired;
  I promise I'll go to sleep early tonight.

I'm sorry I just want to lay around;
  I promise we can go out tomorrow.

I'm sorry I don't want to have sex;
  I promise I'll want to in the morning.

I'm sorry the dirty clothes are piling up;
  I promise I'll do laundry this weekend.

I'm sorry if I
"seemed better" on Monday;
      I promise I'll be "better"
            by Wednesday.

I'm sorry I'm not the person
you fell in love with;
  I promise we'll get back there.

I'm sorry you miss the person
I once was;
  I promise I miss that person too.

(That last one I actually mean.)

Currently listening to:
"All Along" by Kid Cudi

Track Forty-Eight

You are so cautious
when it comes to me;
you stop texting once you've had
too much to drink
to avoid saying things
you really mean.
It could be time
just wasn't on our side,
but if we're being honest,
neither were we.

I should say
"enough is enough"
because walking away
is better in the long run
and one night with you
won't change our outcome.
But then you look at me
like I'm all you see,
and maybe I don't want to be
the strong one.

So, what do you think?
Do we leap from this brink
or let these feelings sink?
Like pennies buried in car seats,
like tears smeared between blinks.

Maybe I should distance
myself from you;
but before I do,
come closer,
I want you more than closure.

What do you think?

Currently listening to:
"Someday You'll Hate Me" by Christopher Andrews

Track Forty-Nine

I joined the Mile Cry Club en route to
Portland. Hovering 30,000 feet over
everything makes even the most chaotic
life look like nothing but a dazzling
mother-of-the-bride dress.

It's a false sense of freedom.

Momentarily, I'm a golden-winged
warbler, with crisis sonar warning me to
soar away before shit hits the fan.

But storm avoidance and crafty flight
patterns are just momentary,
manufactured exhales.

And like that tiny bird,
it's always a round trip back home
to things I need to face
once the worst of it passes.

Currently listening to:
"In the Blood" by John Mayer

Track Fifty

Thunder rolls.
Boats begin to dance.
Pieces of me litter this coast.

Each time I'm here
I swear my heels seep into the sand a
little bit more.

This place is still trying to swallow me
whole.

I tell you that returning feels like
visiting my own grave and you finally
understand why I only come back
on holidays and milestones, with
flowers in my hands.

If the tide has the right to ebb and flow,
to come and go, so do I.

Currently listening to:
"Castle on the Hill" by Ed Sheeran

Track Fifty-One

You died, and I survived.

You died, and I became a person
you will never meet.

Someone you would not have
recognized on the street.

And that's what I can't shake.

You would have never known this
specific incarnation, since I am certain I
am only this person because you left;
someone who would make you proud.

Death gives birth to advocates every
minute. Born again the day you died,
your spirit is alive in everything I do.

We will meet again one day, and you will
be the best, healthiest version of yourself
and I will be the best version of myself
and we will catch up over coffee and
buffalo fries and it will feel as though no
time has passed at all.

That helps me sleep at night.

Currently listening to:
"If You Could See Me Now" by The Script

Track Fifty-Two

I knew you were it when your laugh
made me smile and it took a while, but
we are here now; burning dinners,
swaying to The Spinners.

The way you sleep with one arm over
your head, how you hate that I keep my
socks on in bed. I'd choose us over and
over again.

The small moments,
the slowness, all of it.

Like how I know you chew ice
when you're nervous,
I am certain you are my person.

Our fairytale
is in the details.

Currently listening to:
"Could It Be I'm Falling in Love" by The Spinners

Track Fifty-Three

You gave me the best gift. You left. You left and you didn't come back no matter how much I cried. No matter how much you cried. No matter how many times you got in your car only to turn around before arriving to our past. No matter how many times the wrong headlights in my driveway made my stomach sink. No matter how many times I screamed that you were killing me. No matter how much hearing that killed you. No matter how many times I warned you we were making a mistake. No matter how many times you thought so too. No matter how many unsaid words floated between us in email drafts and half-dialed phone numbers. You gave me the best gift. You broke my heart. You left. And you stayed gone. I want to thank you for that.

Currently listening to:
"Lose You to Love Me" by Selena Gomez

Track Fifty-four

Snowflakes blanket downtown;
it hushes the riot that surrounds—
except the sound of our pounding hearts
that echo through the house.

Martinis shaken dirty;
old records spinning bluesy.
You tiptoe to the window,
say it looks like a movie,
and I have never been so
mesmerized by falling snow.

Three olives for good measure;
we're falling like the weather.
Your cologne on the pillows,
not rushing time together,
letting anticipation grow—
just you and   me,
and the snow.

Currently listening to:
"I've Been Loving You Too Long" by Otis Redding

Track Fifty-Five

You swear your reflection blinked when
you didn't. You've been robotic for quite
some time. Words climb out of your
throat and you don't recognize your
own voice.

You liken yourself to a
failed experiment.

Given light eyes—but a heavy mind.
Given friends—but lonely.

For many years you were told you were
overreacting   lazy   sensitive.

You are none of those things.
You are human and for most of your life

immediacy
was all you knew.

Which made any notion of normalcy
seem fleeting or *not for you.*
Which turned you into an adult
that waits for things to go wrong.
That searches for things to fix.
Which resulted in a worn-out heart
covered in bite marks.

Currently listening to:
"Lonely" by Noah Cyrus

Track Fifty-Six

It's finding the stamps and envelope but missing the energy to drive to the mailbox. It's craving a coffee, traveling fifteen minutes to get it, but then turning around because the place is packed with too many people. It's keeping your gaslight on because you just want to get home and can't imagine making another stop. It's messing up dinner, then crying because it's obviously the end of the world. It's being tired all day, then your head hits the pillow, and you're awake. It's wanting to make plans. It's wanting to return that text. It's wanting to call someone. It's wanting to be how everyone expects you to be. It's that nagging on the tip-of-your-tongue feeling, but you just can't find the words so you feel defective. And it's all of that happening in just one day.

Currently listening to:
"Anxiety" by Julia Michaels
(featuring Selena Gomez)

Track Fifty-Seven

Every time you tuck my hair behind my ear, or cradle my face between your palms, I think you want to tell me you are falling in love with me. Every time you look at me and your eyes become a little sad, I think you want to tell me you are falling in love with me. Every time you kiss my hand or forehead or cheek, I think you want to tell me you are falling in love with me. Every time you stare at me until I look away, I think you want to tell me you are falling in love with me. Every time there is a stretch of silence that would make any other two people uncomfortable, I think you want to tell me you are falling in love with me.

Or maybe I have it backward.
Maybe I am the one
who wants to tell you.

Currently listening to:
"Pushing Up Daisies (Love Alive)" by Brothers Osborne

Track Fifty-Eight

I sit alone on a bench
in Independence Park.
My regret and loneliness
keep me company
as children make believe
the sprinkler is a harp;
the unknowing orchestrators
of my symphony.

I ask myself
as I look down at my sleeves,
what type of person
can simply love and leave?
At the drop of a dime, without a sign.

And the air sighs and sings:
The leaving kind, ma'am,
the leaving kind can.

When did I resign
to become the leaving kind?
I wasn't looking to inflict hurt,
to feed you ground
and know it was dirt.
I wasn't looking to leave you behind,
but I have become the leaving kind.

I need to know why
I still ache and grieve
when I was the one
who decided to leave.
At the drop of a dime,
without a sign.

And the air sighs and sings:
The leaving kind, ma'am,
are allowed to be sad.

Currently listening to:
"Always Be My Baby" by Mariah Carey

Track Fifty-Nine

We may walk the same earth,
but we inhabit very different worlds.
We all take in oxygen,
but the air tastes different
on our tongues.
We are all just passing through
each other's lives,
as visitors, tourists.
We only see what is presented,
offered up.

Some people cannot fathom the notion
of not truly knowing anything
about a person.
Strangers orbiting my world
think they know
what it's like to land,
stick down a flag, and live here.

What fools!

To think they can survive
a day in my ecosystem,
when I often find myself lost
in the uncharted territory
of my own existence.

What fools!

To think they are within reach
of the truth,
when they are lightyears
from my reality.

Currently listening to:
"Conversation Pt. 1" by Mac Miller

Track Sixty

I've always been more prose than poetry, more open-ended than happy ending.

I read book acknowledgments first because I like to know who the author had in their heart when they wrote the book.

I respect people who order their coffee extra hot or with light ice because I think they know exactly what they want out of life. I find it sexy when a person knows how to parallel park. There might be nothing smoother.

I don't think socks have to match and that it's silly that so many spend so much of their limited time on earth folding them together, or searching for their matches, like socks could have a sole mate. I appreciate puns.

I am at a point in my life when I want more authenticity, less brand. More honesty, less beating perimeters of bushes to death.

You miss me?
Tell me.
You want me?
Tell me.

Because I am tired of moonlighting as
the person who's not in love with you.

You're hurting?
Tell me.
You're worried?
Tell me.

Because it's nice and human to have
these things in common.

Currently listening to:
"Someone Who Loves Me" by Sara Bareilles

Track Sixty-One

When you and I first met,
I was depressed and
you were underdressed,
but sitting across from you,
I swear I knew it then.

Now my fingers are running
through your hair.
Your hands, they feel like
coming home.
It's like they've always
belonged here.

Views of the Hudson River,
setting sun and French fries.
My favorite things to borrow
are you and time.

The City is twenty-two miles
past our breeze
but its lights feel warm,
within reach,
as if it could wash up on the beach.

Nothing, nothing
but hazel and blue—
the smell of your shampoo.
Nothing, nothing
but me and you—
so overdue.

Currently listening to:
"Oh Sarah" by Sturgill Simpson

Track Sixty-Two

It's easy to feel out of place lately.
Like you're a day behind everyone else
or in the wrong decade altogether.
Maybe this is just a symptom of a larger
virus. The disease of living through a
shitty time.

We are from the generation that wishes
it were from another generation.
The calluses on our brains are
indicative of having survived a draining
time that we once feared would just
keep replaying.

If we weren't built to endure loss,
we'd sure as hell be dead by now.

But we are still here.
We are still fucking here.

Currently listening to:
"What Do You Stand For" by Olivia Castriota

Track Sixty-Three

I'm nothing but
a product
of my environment
and that's what you don't get.
My wit is a weapon I keep sharp.
I lock the doors behind
myself immediately,
fasten the wrought-iron bars
across my heart.
I don't trust easily.
I'm a species, endangered.
I look over my shoulder.
I don't speak to strangers,
I'm way too in tune with the danger.
If you manage to make it inside,
take what you want,
but leave me my life.

Currently listening to:
"Fate" by H.E.R.

Track Sixty-Four

He had to convince the pharmacist
that he disposed of his old amoxicillin
before she handed over the new script,
but the cashier didn't bat an eye
when he spent $75 at the liquor store.

Her driver's license
had to be scanned by the man
to buy over-the-counter pills,
but the cashier didn't think twice
when she spent $90 at the liquor store.

Currently listening to:
"Drug Dealer" by Macklemore
(featuring Ariana DeBoo)

Track Sixty-Five

I loved you too much.

"Strangers" is the wrong word for what
this is because we knew each other on a
molecular level.

You knew I had a calcium deposit on
my pinky nail and that I considered
three-tined forks pointless and that my
foot twitched whenever I got tired.

I knew you only ate the filling of Oreos
and took two hours to write a three-
sentence email and brushed your teeth
seven times a day.

You may be a "stranger" now, but your
mouth has covered every inch of my
body and I still recognize your
deodorant on the person in front of me
at the bank and I hear your belly laugh
rattle through my entire being when
something supremely funny happens.

I loved you too much.

Being strangers isn't enough distance
for me. I can't unmeet you. Let's call this
what *this* is—you're more of a ghost
than a stranger.

I loved you too much.

Currently listening to:
"It Must Have Been Love" by Roxette

Track Sixty-Six

I haven't flipped the calendar since August / I just want to pause it / I got wrapped up trying to catch up from my time away / Barely caught my breath today / I was a bit disheveled but my mental state stayed level against my throbbing temple / It's perplexing / Because there's always a next thing that keeps me neglecting / What should matter more to me / Like my family and my REM cycle / It's easy to become unbridled / The world has gone crazy / Our vision's gone hazy / I need to stop and smell the daisies to ease my mind / I am worried about mankind / That we're going to run out of time / And soon / Maybe it's the full moon that's got me feeling unbalanced / I mean no malice / My brain is delicate and bruised / Not a bomb that needs to be defused.

Currently listening to:
"That's How I Knew" by Nipsey Hussle

Track Sixty-Seven

Life will toss you things harder to
transform than lemons. Sometimes life
will hand you things that will set your
hands on fire. And my world has been
on fire before. Limited visibility. Only
seeing the moment in front of me.

DO NOT ASK ME WHAT I AM DOING
NEXT WEEK. I DO NOT KNOW.

Don't light that match! I am covered in
gasoline; can't you smell it?

Heat rising from my toes to my throat.
Spending weeks, months, inhaling ash
from the dysfunction, coughing from
the smoke.

Picking out funeral dresses, making sure
it's something I would never want to
wear again.

Taking sleeping pills, because if I wake
up after noon, there are fewer hours in the
day for something terrible to happen.

Putting my phone on silent. Only check it when I know I could handle bad news.

Screaming.
Vomiting.
Praying.
So much praying.
Crying.
So much crying.

If water extinguishes most fires, tell me why my tears singe my face. Tell me why the streaks remain—burns upon my cheeks. If what doesn't kill me will really make me stronger, tell me why I still can't gather my strength to fight back sometimes.

Currently listening to:
"Inner Demons" by Julia Brennan

Track Sixty-Eight

We thought we'd have it
together by now. Figured out.
But we're still scrambling.
We still go on cold walks without a coat.
We still shut down, prefer to implode.
We still create space
so there's no room to be let down.

Yet, even at our most blue,
we were able to sleep.
So what the fuck is this?
Everything is so loud in this black hole
and voids aren't supposed to
make noise.
So what the fuck is this?

To avoid waking up somber,
I started going to bed sober.
Clear eyes and clarity
replaced disorientation and defeat.

How many bad days
need to add up to equal bad life?
The limit does not exist.
Even the days that you fall backward,
or spin in circles instead of advancing
forward, are made up of twenty-four
hours that turn into tomorrow.

And as long as there is tomorrow,
there is hope.

Currently listening to:
"Confessions of a Dangerous Mind" by Logic

Track Sixty-Nine

I don't mail anything in. Even when I appear disheveled, the wrinkles are deliberate. And still, for every success, I see seventeen setbacks. For every time I feel comfortable in my skin, there are more times I wish I could unzip my flesh and step out of my body entirely.

We have all heard the phrase "point of no return." We have convinced ourselves this point exists. The point where there are no take-backs or second chances. I'm here to say that's bullshit. Never give up. You can always turn back, start over, forgive yourself.

Reset. Recalibrate. Reincarnate.

The spectrum of dark and light is vast, but not unforgiving. I have been on both ends. I didn't create a home in my rock bottom, and I hope this year's summit won't be my life's highest peak.

A few years ago, my parents began writing, "The best is yet to come," in my birthday cards.

This has become my prayer.

Currently listening to:
"What a Wonderful World" by Louis Armstrong

Track Seventy

I remember when you wrote, *I will fix us,* on the mirror with the shower steam. I memorized your handwriting before the moment left through the cracked window with the rest of the mist, making the promise dissolve like all your other promises. I knew soon enough that mirror would become just another mirror again. I smiled one of those smiles you only have when you are more sad than happy, and rushed back into bed with you before that bed became just another bed again too.

Currently listening to:
"You and I" by Foxygen

Track Seventy-One

Your lips are softer
than I imagined them to be,
as if they have never
been kissed with urgency.

(Until now.)

This loving, this "you and me,"
tell me that it's better
than you even dreamed,
because I've never been one
to exit gracefully.
So, I hope, you are somewhere
I can stay for at least one more day.

Or for always.

(Either way,
                    I love you.)

Currently listening to:
"Delicate" by Taylor Swift

Track Seventy-Two

I've missed trains
I've been on time for,
waiting on other people
to meet me on the platform.

I will never know how my life
would have turned out if
I had arrived on time.

Maybe, that was the point all along:

to never hear
a shrieking clock and choke,
because time is
nothing but a universal joke.

Currently listening to:
"That's Life" by Frank Sinatra

Track Seventy-Three

Once, the shower heat escaped the bathroom and I just wished it would burn the house down. That was where I was at. I had never been so fucking tired before. I was falling apart more that I wasn't. I wrote the saddest poem of my life sitting on a sunny beach in the Hamptons. I hadn't showered for three days and was taking shit to sleep when I got the call about my first book deal. I got into an argument with you in the middle of Broome Street because I was "always sad" and my "sadness" had begun to seep into other things, like your life.

I wanted to scream back that if you had gone through what I had, you would be worse off. A hermit. Maybe dead. Your peripheral pain was just a graze compared to my wounds. But I was too defeated to care about winning a drunken fight in SoHo. So I hailed a cab.

I wanted to tell you that night on Broome Street that I didn't choose agony. It chose me. I chose to survive though. I chose to welcome happiness with open arms when it would momentarily shine through, like sunlight through curtains. I chose coping skills and scary conversations and recovery.

Currently listening to:
"Appointments" by Julien Baker

Track Seventy-Four

If I am being honest, I knew you weren't the one a few weeks in when you bit directly into a string cheese. I knew, and yet, I allowed you to continue to go against my grain and take up space for 410 days.

The first time we kissed I didn't know you were allergic to Red Dye 40 and I had been eating Swedish Fish by the handful. Within seconds, your tongue and lips became swollen and your face reddened. I don't even like that candy, but I was nervous and needed something to do with my mouth and hands.

We weren't right for a bunch of other, more fatal, serious, non-hypoallergenic reasons too, but sometimes it's that simple.

String-cheese-simple.

Everyone used to say how great we looked together. As if looking great and fitting together were one and the same. When I finally left, my friends asked me why.

I told them that every time I was driving us somewhere, you would alert me whenever someone was in my blind spot. You would grab the oh-shit handle, your knuckles would turn white, and scream that someone was in the next lane. Even when I had no intention of switching lanes.

I knew that if you couldn't trust me to get us somewhere safely a mile up the road, you were never going to trust me with the bigger stuff. And anyone who is with me long enough will no doubt see the bigger stuff. Now I am in your blind spot — now you will never see me again.

Currently listening to:
"Truth Hurts" by Lizzo

Track Seventy-Five

I used to think moths were butterflies
that had grown old.

I used to think birds sang because they
were happy.

Used to think chemo was a cure.

Used to think rain came from holes in
clouds.

That the moon could only be seen at
night.

That *I love you* meant *I'll stay.*

Straw homes are built from
misconceptions. We adapt to the drafts
that whistle through these false truths
until we see them for what they really
are, wolves dressed in delusions' clothing.

I used to think only textbook alcoholics
should stop drinking.

I used to think rest was the natural state
of all objects; that everything that
moves will eventually come to a stop.

But the makeup of my mind runs on
and on and on, even when I plead for a
pause.

I used to think a lot of things,
until I began to live and learn and know.

Currently listening to:
"Hollywood's Bleeding" by Post Malone

Track Seventy-Six

By the time you text me your regret,
I am already eastbound and down.
You never thought I would leave.
Well, neither did I.

I always bought the ticket but never got
on the plane. I always imagined moving
on, but my feet remained entangled
with our ruins.

I always kept the million reasons I had
to walk away packed haphazardly in
my go-bag. Nothing momentous
happened the day I actually left. There
was no big fight, no grand reveal.

There was just me and the echo of my
footsteps, walking around a house
that didn't feel like home anymore.

Currently listening to:
"I Didn't Belong" by Highland Kites

Track Seventy-Seven

Making a living off your brain could make you lose your mind / Too busy looking for lost time that I end up running behind / I drift from cookie-cutter conversation / I dream about airports and train stations / Of deconstructing rumors and fabricated reputations / In some remote location / Fears only eat what they are fed / So instead, I starved mine to death / Got cozy with the monsters inside my head and began to sleep beside them beneath my bed / If they were going to haunt me, figured we might as well be friends / Ghouls are just doubts we give life to / We make them too real, forget they are see through / I'll see this through / Like I always do.

Currently listening to:
"Take Me Down" by Mista Encore

Track Seventy-Eight

People, places, and things
have broken my heart
over and over and over again.
In the process of fighting
to keep it beating
over and over and over again,
I changed.

Now, the monster under my bed
falls asleep before I do.

The bones in my closet turn to powder
waiting for me to hang up clothes
I washed two weeks ago.

The ghosts in my town have vacated,
looking for a haunt that's a little less
haunted.

You see
over and over and over again
I chose to live and now I am the
strongest I've ever been.

There are no longer vultures
circling my sky.
I have not been the prey
in quite some time.

Currently listening to:
"HUMBLE." by Kendrick Lamar

Track Seventy-Nine

Now that your lips have been on mine
I wonder how they will feel
other places.
If this is what a fall from grace is,
God, let me keep falling—
because I'm all in.

People who see me say I glow,
like I know something they don't.
I want to remember it all,
so I could miss it if it goes.

God, let me keep falling—
because I'm all in.
All in.

I'll write about us
until the words no longer fit.

I am all in.
All in.

Currently listening to:
"I'll Be Seeing You" by Billie Holiday

Track Eighty

We are all made
of water and pain.
Both are necessary.
Neither is poison.

You had to show up for others
for a long time.
Be a safe harbor. A therapist.
A mediator.
An encyclopedia. A lighthouse.

Aftermaths became cozy.

You let others cry, vent, scream.
All the while, your pain was bubbling to
the surface and there'd be this
screeching-teapot ringing in your ears.
You would pull into a CVS parking lot
or run the shower and cry in secret.
You'd scream internally or into a pillow.

Then answer your phone like you hadn't
been up for two days straight.
Not because others expected you to
never have your own breakdowns.
But because you sincerely thought if
they saw you crumble,
they would crumble even more and you
didn't want that for them.

You wanted them to get better.
So, you stayed quiet.
And let it destroy you
from the inside, out.

Let those years serve as a learning
moment. You'll never stop showing up
for people, but you'll never put yourself
through it that way again.

We are in repair, never beyond repair.
We are healing, never healed.

Currently listening to:
"Life to Come" by The Killers

Track Eighty-One

When you're *other,* you will lose time.
You will be less reason, more rhyme.
You will self-medicate your mind
to ease the havoc and clutter.
You'll sleep alone in the gutter.
Your light will crackle the sky,
you'll disrupt like thunder.
When you're *other.*

When your eyes see the world
in an obscure way,
opinions of the majority will sway,
but hardly land in your favor.

When you can make beauty
out of your pain,
you'll be an outsider until you decay,
then they'll call you a trailblazer.

When you're *other,*
it is easy to feel alone,
though you feel you're best
on your own.
It's easy to find yourself lost,
when your faith and trust
have been crossed.
Easy to question your sanity
when your art stems from tragedy.

When you're *other,*
the world will seem overcrowded
by perceptions that are clouded.
You will yearn for a safe haven,
a forest of creation.
Then, a place will call out to you:
"You are *other,* run for cover."

It's a place
to breathe new breath.
To gather strength.
To reach new lengths.
To shut your eyes
and count to ten.

It's a place to dance with
the skeletons in your closet,
take turns waltzing with
the reasons that caused this.
As they stretch their bones
and regrow their flesh,
you will thank them for
creating this mess.

Because here, you will find your peace
in who you are, in how you think,
in how you see things differently.
And at the top of your lungs
you will sing:

"I am *other*, one of a kind.
There are no flaws in my design.
You cannot keep me confined.
Stars seek me out to sleep over.
Even in dark, I find color.
I will raise up those who suffer.
I search for rain, not for cover.
My light will adorn the sky,
I'll erupt like thunder.
I am *other*."

Currently listening to:
"All My Favorite People" by Maren Morris
(featuring Brothers Osborne)

Track Eighty-Two

Ice patches float on top of the lake like lily pads do in the muggy months. The wind has not been able to budge the water for weeks and is making up for lost time.

Snow dusts the surrounding pines, reminding me of the small artificial trees my great-grandmother used to meticulously place within her miniature Christmas village. It's the type of beautiful that I know my cracked screen won't replicate, so when I show people later, they won't understand why I was so captivated.

I don't feel this serene often. My changing of seasons was not as graceful as this; no one would have stopped and appreciated what they saw. It was more akin to being eaten alive by fire ants. Dragonflies would often land on my chest or elbows during this time: an omen of things to come.

There is no growth without breakage, nothing to salvage without a wreckage to scour. I survived wounds my therapist warned could prove fatal, and today I got to see the most beautiful lake begin to thaw back to life right before my eyes.

Currently listening to:
"Lua" by Bright Eyes

Track Eighty-Three

I place my ear to a shell and know that
the crashing I hear inside isn't the ocean.
I can see why children believe it is, but
it's just the resonating air producing
sound.

You have a ribcage like a conch shell.

I put my ear to your chest, and I think I
hear you falling in love; but it's just the
pump of your heart producing sound.

We hear what we want to hear.

Currently listening to:
"I'm Goin' Down" by Mary J. Blige

Track Eighty-Four

The past is not something we can simply place down on a coffee table or leave behind at an airport. The past is a part of us; sometimes for better, mostly for worse, but a part of us nonetheless. To think we can simply "let go" of the past is just as silly as thinking we need to offer up who we are today as sacrificial lambs in order to become who we will be tomorrow. It's all so tethered and rooted that it feels fluid.

We cannot fully "let go," not really. We can't forget, not completely. But we can accept some things will always look more picturesque—seem more serene—from a safe distance, from a faint recollection, and we can move forward. It is imperative that we always move forward.

Currently listening to:
"That Was Yesterday" by Leon Bridges

Track Eighty-Five

I had a nightmare we were still together.
I needed you but your phone was dead.
Or in your car. Or on someone else's
nightstand.

-I WOKE UP TIRED-

Even in a dreamworld,
your bullshit exhausts me.
Even in a dreamworld,
you can't show up for me.
Even in a dreamworld,
we would never work out.

The nightmare is no longer
perpetual, though.

-I GET TO WAKE UP-

Currently listening to:
"Rain on Me" by Ashanti

Track Eighty-Six

We live in a world where guns and the flu are killing children whose older siblings are already dying off from heroin and fentanyl and other drugs their parents explain away to them by saying, "She took too much medicine and lives in Heaven now."

We live in a world where when I ask a ten-year-old what he wants to be when he grows up, instead of saying an astronaut or firefighter or president, he just replies, "Here. I still want to be here when I grow up."

And I know by *here* he means *alive*.

And I wonder when understanding the fragility of one's mortality was lumped in with teaching fractions and cursive and the state capitals.

And, with two decades between us, I look into his eyes and they look older than mine. My heart breaks at his statement and tears roll down my face but he doesn't understand why, because there are two decades between us, and he is still only a child.

Currently listening to:
"Waterfalls" by TLC

Track Eighty-Seven

Be like water. Fill every space like it was made just for you, like you belong there. Yes, there's a risk you'll pour over and soak whatever is near, but water doesn't worry about what it wets; it just flows or falls. Water doesn't apologize, and most days it just dries, melts, or freezes like it was never there. But sometimes it leaves a mark behind—it all depends on what it touches. Don't be afraid to leave behind a mark. Be like water.

Currently listening to:
"Carry On" by Norah Jones

Track Eighty-Eight

I spend so much time trying to outrun who I once was that I sometimes throw away the notion that there are pieces of me worth salvaging.

Like the part of me that always pauses for a sunset. The part that watches fireworks, lips parted in awe. The part that walks the shoreline and collects shells for my mother. The part that tries to catch soapy bubbles on my fingertips. The part that hasn't eaten meat in years, but still thinks of my childhood home whenever I smell bacon.

The part of me that decorates three trees and remains enchanted by Christmas lights. The part of me that acts surprised whenever my nephew finds me in a game of hide and seek.

These parts—not my job or my weight or my clothes or the size of my house—are the parts of me that if I were to lose, I'd lose touch with myself and begin

f
l
o
a
t
i
n
g

lost   in   space.

Currently listening to:
"Watching the Wheels" by John Lennon

Track Eighty-Nine

The lights blink amber,
the street signs are down.
Another summer over
for this seaside town.

Things haven't been the same
since the hurricane came.
It's been two years since I've
stepped into the arcade.
At one point in my life,
I used to go there every day.

The Exxon is gone,
the paint has chipped off the chapel.
Catch in my lungs,
never enough oxygen in a time capsule.

The lights blink amber,
the street signs are down.
Another summer over
for this seaside town.

Currently listening to:
"Glory Days" by Bruce Springsteen

Track Ninety

You try to count up how many versions
of yourself were sacrificed in exchange
for the person you are today.
You lose track after running out of
fingers and toes and those
tiny tiles on the bathroom wall.
Stop trying to reverse-engineer
what brought you here.
The iterations do not matter.
What matters is that you shed skin
trusting that you'd never reach bone.
What matters is you cried tears,
knowing that you wouldn't drown.
What matters is you believed others
when they told you that you mattered.

What matters is you
kept believing
you mattered too.

Currently listening to:
"On to the Next One" by Jay-Z
(featuring Swizz Beatz)

Track Ninety-One

The stillness inside of me is gone,
leaked through my ears and tear ducts.
That's what happens when the weight
of the world leaves your shoulders and
enters your head.

I no longer can sit silent with myself.
I pace. Race. Twitch. Itch.
Did I leave the stove on?
Did I blow out that candle?
Did I lock the door?
Better go back and check.

There will always be things to fix,
to obsess over.
The worries are infinite;
the days are finite.

This life.
This world as you know it right now,
filled with the people you love,
will be gone one day.

So, when you feel the sadness lingering,
remember not every guiding light
will glow bright.
There is a lesson found
in all your days,
even hidden in the
worst ones of your life.

Carry on, carry on.

Currently listening to:
"Let It Matter" by JOHNNYSWIM

Track Ninety-Two

I know you need me to need you.
Visibly. Obviously. Irrevocably.

But I've lived without things
I've needed to live
for such a long time.
My ability to mend
after something ends is uncanny.

I know tears dry.
I know smiles return.
I know the sun rises and life rolls on.
Even when it feels like it won't,
it always does.

Because when one thing stops,
the rest doesn't.
And the rest can be so good
that you begin to call it the beginning.

Currently listening to:
"Settling Down" by Miranda Lambert

You have reached
the end of Side A.

SIDE B

The remixes.

Track One

I tell you I feel tired
and you say,
"But you slept for twelve hours,"
and I knew you didn't get it.

I tell you maybe I need Vitamin D
and you crack a joke about your dick;
and I knew you didn't get it.

You tell me I have
"nothing to be sad about."
I agree and you meet me with a shrug;
and I knew you didn't get it.

I tell you the noise and the crowd are
getting to me and you say, "I told you
that you didn't have to come;"
and I knew you didn't get it.

I tell you my temples feel heavy
and you say, "Take Advil;"
and I knew you didn't get it.

You suggest maybe another shower,
or makeup,
or a run will lift my spirits,
and I knew you didn't get it.

I tell you, and tell you,
and tell you and you never get it.
Don't worry.
It's not your fault . .

I get it.

Currently listening to:
"Fix You" by Coldplay

Track Two

No one knows how much she cried last Wednesday. Because 'she still hit her marks. She got out of bed, though she did off the covers. She showered but forgot to rinse out the conditioner. She put on clean clothes, though they were a bit wrinkled.

There were no runs in her tights, no mascara clumps by her eyes. She was only five. minutes late, which is considered "on time" when you're running on four hours of sleep and Seasonal Depression. She didn't engage in conversation but greeted everyone with a smile. She went home without an appetite but still cooked dinner. She had sex but didn't finish.

No one knows how much she cried last Wednesday because she was quiet about it, and to some, pain is only noticed when it is public, and loud, and obvious. No one knows how much she cried last Wednesday be a Thursday w better and, by then, she didn't want to dwell on yesterday.

Currently listening to:
"Speed Trap Town" by Jason Isbell

Track Three

We may sleep together,
but my dreams are my own.

That's always been my problem. I shut
people out. I only let them see me from
certain angles, in certain lighting, at
certain moments. My mother says it's
because I am independent. My therapist
says it's my defense mechanism. My ex
says it's why we broke up. My friends
say they love me anyway.

I say it's because I feel
safest in half measures.

I'll love you—but not completely.
I'll hold your hand—but won't
interlace our fingers.
I'll take pictures—but won't tag you.
I'll miss you—but never enough to ever
question leaving.

Currently listening to:
"Pushin' Time" by Miranda Lambert

Track Four

For now, I will say
I wanted to take a picture
of you in the car.
The sun was setting
and there was this tugging on my heart,
telling me I was going to want
to remember this part.

But I knew a photo
wouldn't live up to
what my eyes were living,
so I just stared at you
until the sun disappeared
behind a building.

For now, I will say
when we were walking
around the harbor,
if it weren't for the people
with umbrellas running for cover
I would have never felt the rain
or heard the thunder.

And if you knew what my mind
was like before,
you'd get what I meant
that grey day
when I said you were the only one
who could make me forget
it was pouring.

Currently listening to:
"Them Changes" by Thundercat

Track Five

I don't tell you that I went to work today in the shirt I slept in last night. I don't tell you that I cried on the couch for no ▓▓ r▓ason.

▓▓▓▓▓▓ o▓▓▓▓▓▓ m hungover in the middle of the week. I don't tell you I can't recall the last time my mind didn't hurt.

I don't need to tell you any of this for you to sense that burnout is imminent. You don't need to know the whole story to understand the story.

That is why you are beautiful

You tell me you are here if I want to talk. You tell me I better sleep tonight because the bags under my eyes are atrocious. You tell me I better eat and take an iron pill.

I don't push back. I sincerely t▓▓ ▓▓ that I am trying. You believe me, and you believe in me. And that's the precarious, precious cycle that keeps me going.

Thank you for not needing the whole story to understand the story.

Currently listening to:
"Closer to Love" by Mat Kearney

Track Six

I implore you

crawl out of that grave
before the dust settles
before the grass returns.

Before you get too comfortable
with death, with oblivion.
Before your fingerprints
the footprints are wiped clean.
Before the world
gets used to spinning without you.

You're too priceless
to remain lifeless
in cheap pine.
In a dress you didn't choose.
In caked-on makeup.
You never slept well on your back.

Break your nails.
Scuff your knuckles.
Claw the ground.
Bloom.

You belong here on the surface,
with pomegranate and tulip poplar
trees, with traffic and lavender and
morning breath.

Not wherever comes next.
Not yet.

Not on a day like this and
when
your existence stops to exist.

Currently listening to:
"Wake Me Up (Acoustic)" by AVICII
(featuring Aloe Blacc)

Track Seven

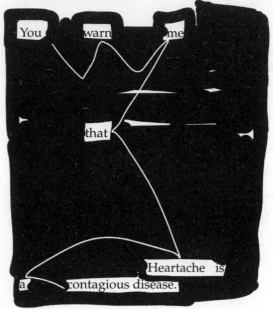

You warn me
that
Heartache is
a contagious disease.

Currently listening to:
"Back to Black" by Amy Winehouse

Track Eight

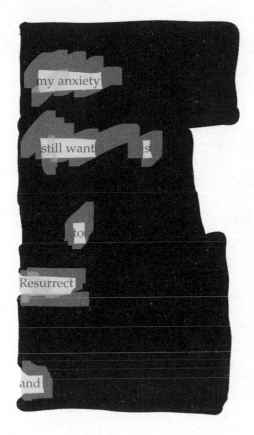

my anxiety

still want   s

to

Resurrect

and

Replay

moments

every night.

Currently listening to:
"Slow It Down" by Mike Posner

Track Nine

We were too b s   vive the
                              what it
                          en split
op

We were too busy chasing survival that
we didn't even consider tha   s of
surviving and restoring woul hurt oo.

We were too   gid tombs,
not worrying a   n d eds, dirty
dishes, or ke   r, that we
forgot that normalcy gives off warmth.

We were too busy   king up broken
glass that we n   our trauma,
started to liken th gather g of shards to
collecting shells   the shore, or
inspecting snowflakes; each one unique
in its sharpness   deadliness.

We were too bu y bsessing over how
something w   ou dn't ask for in one
million   ye   ould   show   up
unannounced and dictate our live in a
such a way, that our memories ecam
distorted, or amplified, or wen missing
altogether.

We were too busy drawing lines in the
sand and biting tongues and preparing
for war, that we   ot that once upon a
time there was a peace.

Currently listening to:
"America's Sweetheart" by Elle King

Track Ten

You pupils dilated
when I walked in the room
and I knew I had you.

I used to wonder what it'd be like
to kiss you at midnight.
Now we share the same
bar of soap in the shower
and I wake up in love with you.
I kiss your face
where a strip of sunlight
touches your cheek every morning.

It's as though you're not just the love of
my life, but the love of all my lifetimes.
Like we've been here before,
like we'll be here again.

And again. And again.
Looping in a way
that doesn't make me dizzy.

Currently listening to:
"Stay" by Mac Miller

Track Eleven

Sometimes I feel like I only feel anything
wh██ ██ thing ██ going wrong;
that I only drive this far down the
turnpike when I am losing my mind.

My tires mold to the familiar roads back
to my old lif█ ████████ muscle memory
replaces the need for GPS; where you
██████ ███ ██████ ██ have to go right;
where there exist people who can
reintrod█████ ████ to myself.
I trust th██ ██ ███ I trust with my life can
help bring me back to life.

Because no one now
knew me at my best.
My old friends were there
before the detonator blew.
They hold me ████ ██ me in
time-traveling truth,
and there is comfort.

Currently listening to:
"Sweet As Whole" by Sara Bareilles

Track Twelve

We've started to hold our breath
in a world of breathable air.
Hands as raw as Lady Macbeth;
when love is war, all is not fair.

When you had
you loved and
I wish you had said
that you loved me instead.

We've confused passion and pain,
turned each other into liars.
We have become colliding trains;
no survivors, no survivors.

Currently listening to:
"Everybody Lost Somebody" by Bleachers

Track Thirteen

I brush my teeth
and overthink
over the sink.
There are layers to loving me
and most of them aren't pretty.

My reflection doesn't compute.
I don't look like a girl
who has nothing to lose
but I feel like one — I've come undone.

It's the nature of my beast;
I care the most or I care the least,
never ever in between.

Fuzzy pictures to match my life,
could never get the focus right.
Caught up in moving on or staying put;
looking forward, stealing a second look.

So the story always goes,
I'm your soulmate or your foe,
writer's blocked or on a roll.

My heart isn't conditioned
to listen
to anything but its own beat.
There are layers to loving me;
but to the naked eye, I
am just here brushing my teeth.

Currently listening to:
"In Between" by Kelsea Ballerini

Track Fourteen

The spring we met,
I was more wilt than bloom.
I'm not saying you saved me,
but your face and eyes and laugh
made me look back long enough to
think twice.

My se   e was quiet;
only I heard it, but you were there
when it happened and that's enough.

How lucky I am
to have stayed long enough
to play with the hair
at the nape of your neck.

To learn the reasons
behind your nail biting
and the scar   s

To feel you twitch
and to have our bare feet
touch in our sleep.

To eat shrimp tacos with you
in front of the television

I would have missed out on so much.
I would have missed out on the person
I became since knowing you.

Currently listening to:
"Good Old Days" by Macklemore
(featuring Kesha)

Track Fifteen

My throat's collecting dust;
I haven't sung in months
So overwhelmed by what I need to do
that my to-do list goes untouched.

I can't hold this pose forever.
My legs are starting to tremor.
It's so damn hard to measure up.

I have scrapes on these knees from
praying too hard
and scrapes on my heart from
staying too long.

Oh, I'm broken,
even dreams take their toll and
I need to regain focus.
Goals come with strings
and when I say I'm tired
you don't get what I mean.

I'm feeling the worst pain.
Just trying to save face.
Sitting in therapy wondering why
I keep getting in my own way.

I am a mosaicked woman,
making choices a bit crooked.
Doing things I really shouldn't do.

I have aches in my brain from
wondering too hard,
and aches in my legs from

I'm only human,

I'm only human,

I'm only human,

Currently listening to:
"Change" by NF

Track Sixteen

a funeral

stopped

traffic
f   or

death

on

a

busy street
and you didn't even know it.

Currently listening to:
"See You Again" by Wiz Khalifa
(featuring Charlie Puth)

Track Seventeen

You're not good today

The light hurts your eyes and you left
the house without washing your face so
it's 2:00 p.m. and you are still wiping
away crust from the corners of your
eyes.

You're not good today.

The weather is affecting your mood and
you are crying too easily at
commercials, so you put on something
you've seen a trillion times.

You're not good today.

You've been tired since you woke up
but your mind won't quiet down
enough to rest, so you light a candle at
3:18 a.m. and decide you'll call your
parents later on in the morning.

You're not good today
and you're good with that.

You understand your mind and your
body; you know even though you're
down you're not down for the count.
You breathe in and out. You will not let
today obstruct the potential in
tomorrow.

Currently listening to:
"Promise of a Rainbow" by Katherine Quintana

Track Eighteen

They ask me again
why I dropped the rose on your coffin
but kept the stem.

Sometimes
time doesn't hold up
its end of the bargain,
and water doesn't
regrow the gardens.
Sometimes time,
try as it might,
can't keep its word
and doesn't heal you
from what occurred.

When they ask me
how long you've been dead,
you die in my head all over again.

Currently listening to:
"Slow Healing Heart" by Dolly Parton

Track Nineteen

For a long time I couldn't shake a snow globe without being reminded of your indiscretions.

The day my eyes watched you leave, my body stayed on the stoop and the first snow of the year started. I remember thinking, *How fucking poetic.*

It never occurred to me that I could stay warm in my skin after what we weathered.

The gusts from the storms of our saga blew scraps of you into my face. You were in photos, in text messages, in strangers, in song lyrics, in certain smells, in clothes of mine I knew you loved.

There is stability in the aftermath of instability. There's beauty in hard transitions.

Though it may seem magical and
swift from the outside, any
transformation can be gruesome deep
inside the chrysalis.

The butterfly would confess this to us if
we understood her language.

By the time the first snow of another
year began to fall without you, and my
street quietly transformed into
something else as I slept, I was okay. I
had become someone different inside of
my familiar skin, and I was okay.

This is still a love poem
even if I don't love you anymore.

Currently listening to:
"Brand New Me" by Alicia Keys

Track Twenty

I ~~never or gotten~~ used to seeing
my family be a family without me on
the internet

My own absence barely fazes me;
because the less post ~~the more I~~ reveal
and the less I scroll, the better I feel.

I am worried about the state of art.

      IT'S

           ALL TOO

                        STATE OF
                        THE ART.

It's surface level,
nothing to it:
elevator music.

Currently listening to:
"High Time" by Kacey Musgraves

Track Twenty-One

As we kiss in the car, I find my███lf
purpose██ inhali███████████ deep
i█to my lungs. I know I need to take in
as much of you as I can.

"Let's g█ watch █he sunset████ s█ggest,
putting the car in gear.

"Are we going to ███e it?" I ask,
peering out the █ind█w as the
sun dips behind the trees.

"Yeah. Definitely██ you answer.

I let you go on believing that I am asking
about the sunset.

Currently listening to:
"Landslide" by Fleetwood Mac

Track Twenty-Two

Nervous, uncertain,
rambling, but wordless;
the pain, it immersed us.

You got the broom and swept up the
glass and broken trust.
Found needles from the cedar from our
last happy Christmas.

The hatchets we planted
in the dead of winter
bloomed in June.

That's the thing about civil wars,
they're always more personal.
That's the thing about closed doors,
they're always more confessional.
That's the thing about hearts like yours,
they're just so damn merciful.

Currently listening to:
"If You Came Back from Heaven" by Lorrie Morgan

Track Twenty-Three

The creatures from my deep won't stay
submerged forever.

They will surface and sing or scream.
They will touch sunlight and bask or
burn.

And I will have no control
over any of this.

It happens suddenly.
I could be fine for days, weeks, months.

Until I am not.

Reminiscences and tears
are bees that sting.
Suddenly. Quickly.
Maybe not even on purpose.
First instinct is to swat,
but I know they'll be extinct one day
and I can't yet imagine a world where
these memories don't sporadically
buzz through my bramble brain.

I brush up against a memory,
ever so briefly, accidentally.
And the wound reopens.

Today, I took a sip of cucumber water
but tasted my past and was reminded
that you don't have to deliberately
pick at a scab for it to bleed.

Currently listening to:
"Patiently Waiting" by 50 Cent
(featuring Eminem)

Track Twenty-four

Currently listening to:
"Dead (Acoustic)" by Madison Beer

Track Twenty-five

There is still snow on the ground and you can't for the life of you recall the last time you saw snow this far along in the spring. But soon, the time will come for dodging dripping air conditioners that hang from windows that will never know central air. The cash-only ice cream parlor will open for the season in a few short weeks. The warmth is coming even though all you can feel is cold right now. The ice you nearly slipped on in the parking lot this morning is nothing but a puddle come afternoon and will freeze over again once the sun goes to sleep. All of these small things are signs that air shifting and blooming daffodils and songbirds will be here soon.

Currently listening to:
"Here Comes the Sun" by The Beatles

Track Twenty-Six

I'm in my own head a lot.

Last night you caught me staring at the
wall for far too long. Sometimes, I can't .
sleep for days, which affects you when
it's 2:47 a.m. and I try to have a
conversation with you, ~~and then~~ that is
when the fog lifts and I am awake.

I forget to call you when I get home and
you get frustrated when I abandon my
shoes in the middle of the room or don't
charge my phone (it's on 8% right now,
so I need to make this quick).

I don't make beds or fold clothes—I'll
wear your socks and boxers to bed. You
sigh really hard each time I don't use a
coaster, but that won't condition me to
care ~~about~~ condensation.

All of this is difficult.
I know.

I am a hard person to love. None of this
makes me eccentric or an enigma or
artistic.

It makes me a
neurotic pain in the ass.

Sparks did not fly when you met me,
those were warning flares,
d i s t r e s s signals.

Currently listening to:
"I Can't Make You Love Me" by Bonnie Raitt

Track Twenty-Seven

They kissed goodbye instead of *see you tomorrow*.

To this day, they wonder if the other detected the subtle differences. Like how they held one another a bit longer, a bit tighter. How they walked away slowly, turning around to ensure that the other's smiling face was burned into their memory. They wonder if the other noticed how the "I love you" that left their lips was their most honest declaration, said slowly and deliberately, because they knew they could never say it again.

Did they hear the slight break in voice? They wonder if the other felt them press close, ear to chest, just to feel the heartbeat through the other's shirt before it broke, healed, and began beating for someone else. They wonder if the other saw how they sat in the car, long after firing up the engine, begging their heart to stop dragging its feet and get in the shotgun seat so they could drive away.

They wonder if the other knows that not everyone who *has* to leave *wants* to leave.

Currently listening to:
"All We Are" by Matt Nathanson

Track Twenty-Eight

Loaded livers and statements
tonight in this basement bar.
Your fingers are too far away.

Trading repartee
between red wine sips.
I catch you staring
at my lips.
Then you joke about
the age difference.

But I have caught up

in decades

and mindsets

and regrets.

In lost games

and upsets

and life tests.

You say that you should go,
but you don't leave your seat.
We brace for our impact
and the flames it will bring.

You and me,
lost and found,
lost and foundering.

Currently listening to:
"The Lonely" by Christina Perri

Track Twenty-Nine

To the untrained eye, these coping mechanisms often look a lot like self-destruction.

The binge drinking. The binge sleeping. The insomnia. The dust on the ceiling fans, the ring around the tub. The wallowing. The nonstop working. The procrastinating. The canceling therapy last minute so they still take your co-pay. The toothpaste spit on the mirror. The phone that hasn't been charged. The *Are you still watching 'The Office'?* prompts. The drives where you can't remember taking the turns but still arriving at the destination. The writer's block. The missed calls and *The mailbox you wish to reach is full* dismissals. The unwashed hair, the un-run dishwasher. The oil splatter that has made itself comfortable on the stove.

It's all needed. Maybe to destroy yourself just enough so your current existence can no longer be sustained. This way, there will be no other choice but to rebuild, to come back as the person you earned the right to become.

Currently listening to:
"You Get What You Give" by New Radicals

Track Thirty

When you meet a writer,
they won't write

You'll kiss and have sex and smile,
and they won't write about you.

You'll fall in love,
befriend each other's friends,
and they won't write about you.

You'll binge-watch shows,
learn how they take their coffee,
and they won't write about you.

You might be together one year,
five years, a decade; dancing together
at weddings and consoling one
another at funerals, and they won't
write about you.

Then it will fall
apart.

You will leave or they will leave, or
you'll both stay and start sleeping back-
to-back, because staying is easier than
leaving, and *that* is when they will write
about you.

Currently listening to:
"Force of Forgetting" by Taylor Belle

Track Thirty-One

Sunglasses are dark,
car's in park—just idling.
My numbness is frightening.

Overthinking again,
biting the inside of my mouth,
picking at my cuticles.

In need of a friend,
lonely living in a world
addicted to pharmaceuticals.

Currently listening to:
"Same Drugs" by Chance the Rapper

Track Thirty-Two

You never appreciate my presence, but you feel my absence in your joints and arteries. In the mornings you wake, eyelids dusted with frost because you were only dreaming of my warmth. Your fantasies were too busy wondering, your hands were too busy reaching in wrong directions to hold onto what mattered. Until what mattered decided you didn't matter. Until what mattered left with a new number and lover and priorities. You never loved me, but your heart broke just the same the day I stopped loving you and began to love myself.

Currently listening to:
"Love Like This" by Ben Rector

Track Thirty-Three

The Devil's making lemonade
out of my dilemmas.
I'm not antisocial—
but I don't speak venom.
It's a slippery slope,
to deny it or cope.
Won't know 'til I hit water
if I will sink or float.

The more you console me,
the lonelier I get.
I know you can't handle
the loose threads in my head.
I must be something to see,
weeping under the willow tree,
trying to get out the knots
in the necklace you gave me.

I leave with the ease
of a traveling, tented show.
I can't see your face,
and your voice I won't recall.
Because the dead keep breathing
only when you let them talk.

But please hold off on the dispatch,
I'm on the mend.
I'll keep my hope in a bottle
so it won't sail off again.

Currently listening to:
"Mad" by Solange
(featuring Lil Wayne)

Track Thirty-four

You think my idiosyncrasies are sexy
until you see them barefaced, no
makeup.

But I AM RUNNING OUT OF
METAPHORS TO MAKE HOW
SHITTY I FEEL more digestible,
quotable, poetic.

My overthinking is only romantic when
it is described as a wanderlust mind that
spans galaxies; not when I call it what it
is, *obsessive and intrusive.*

My tense and achy muscles only hold
appeal when they arrive alongside a
photo of my body.

My tears remain drinkable when the
bloodshot lines burning my eyes match
the stellar patterns of Orion.

Healing is only healing when it's linear
and universal, ended with stardust
and glitter; not when it's inconsistent
and personal, mixed with grit and
couches.

Reality disturbs some of the same
people who plead for authenticity.

*When will they realize they are one and the
same?*

They still try though, to take the literal
out of context. To make pain more
digestible, quotable, poetic.

Pretty, even.
It's none of those things.

Currently listening to:
"everything i wanted" by Billie Eilish

Track Thirty-Five

invite

 thoughts

In

 messy

year.

Currently listening to:
"To Me" by Alina Baraz

Track Thirty-Six

The ~~past has~~ a tendency
to drip out a little at a time,
like water from a loose faucet
in the middle of the night.

Life can be tough
when you've never done well
with ticking clocks
or lights on city blocks
(or ~~????~~ small talk).

The cough syrup at the pharmacy
reminds me of the energy thing
you ~~used to drink~~ when we were young.
When we took ~~those~~ rides
to ~~????~~ with the radio up.
We ~~????~~ ~~we were back~~ then.
We're all scared of who we'll become,
when all is said and done.

Currently listening to:
"Hurt" by Johnny Cash
(Nine Inch Nails' cover)

Track Thirty-Seven

Lately I have been dreaming of another realm outside of this dystopia where "umpteenth" is an actual number and "someday" is a day of the week and "soon" and "eventually" are realistic measurements of time.

A world where wishes can be granted by weeds and stars and flickering candles. A world where you can have the impossible, like time machines for second chances or the hollow bones of a bird to fly away from whatever has hurt you.

I am drained from breathing here, in a world with last words and final hugs, where we have to worry about clocks running out and saying goodbye to people we know we can't live without but will have to one day. It is hard to live in this world of inevitabilities.

Then, the first frost of the season dances up my windows, or the red-winged blackbird flutters back to its branch where leaves have also returned, or the summer sun blazes deep into the evening hours, or the smell from a wood-burning fireplace mixes with the air, and I am no longer weary.

During these soft transitions, when you can taste the faint hint of a rainbow, what truly matters in life rises above all the insignificance to its rightful place on the surface, and what should have always mattered the most becomes what matters most once again.

Currently listening to:
"Do Better" by Ada Pasternak

Track Thirty-Eight

We kiss and my lipstick
ends up on your coffee lid.
The way your breath touches my ear—
we are alone, everywhere.

You don't know what you do for me—
or to me—
the lightning you course through me.
My feet have found solid ground.
Skies have parted—no dark clouds.
You managed to slow me down just
enough to pause, to breathe,
to turn my life around.

And I hope you are still here
this time next year.

We can wake up to change
and we don't have much say
in what breaks our way,
or how long people stay;

but before I met you my mind
and my heart were at odds all the time.
Then you floated in on a dandelion wish
and every since knowing you exist,
I just want to sit, count your eyelashes.

And I hope you are still here
this time next year.

I've never been synonymous
with keeping promises,
but this is different.

If you don't,
then I won't
disappear.

And we'll still be here
this time next year.

Currently listening to:
"Rise Up" by Andra Day

Track Thirty-Nine

~~Things to~~ ~~remember~~ do:

- ~~Move~~ ~~the kitchen~~ ~~the room~~ ~~and~~ ~~shower~~ ~~and~~ ~~holidays.~~
- Smile ~~when~~ ~~they~~ ~~is~~ ~~funny~~ ~~lies.~~
- Wonder why ~~he~~ ~~when~~
- ~~When~~ ~~sleep.~~
- ~~When~~ ~~collect~~ the energy ~~put clothes~~ ~~away~~ ~~in the~~
- ~~Please~~ ~~go~~ ~~Vitamin D~~ ~~deficiency~~
- ~~When~~ ~~Tuesday and~~ ~~going~~ to the gym, ~~but~~ go to therapy.
- Go home ~~and~~ ~~Go home~~ and ~~before~~ ~~rained~~ ~~to~~ charge ~~your~~ ~~phone because~~ ~~w~~ ~~more~~ every day ~~last night~~ ~~exhausts.~~
- ~~and "depression."~~
- ~~memory.~~

Currently listening to:
"Note to Self" by Ben Rector

Track Forty

A lot stay buried under
feet that are stationary.
You said being with me *felt heavy*
and my composure cracked
under the weight of that.

I've developed a habit
of lighting matches
then staying in the room,
taking in the fumes for too long.

I'm not trying to be dramatic,
but these are the facts:
bad habits are stealthy.
I just want to be healthy
and happy with where I'm at.

Currently listening to:
"Someone You Loved" by Lewis Capaldi

Track Forty-One

Our last hug, you lifted me off the
ground like you wanted to take me with
you, like you didn't want to let me go,
but you left me there.

And yet,
when you placed me back on my feet,
my knees didn't buckle.
I remained standing.
That's how I knew that
plot twists don't always have to feel
like the turning of a knife.
They can feel like the bridge
in your favorite song.
They can feel like daylight on your face.
They can feel like a second chance
at a better life.

Currently listening to:
"Victory" by Puff Daddy
(featuring The Notorious B.I.G. & Busta Rhymes)

Track Forty-Two

A month ago, when this was planned, you were excited. Now you are filled with dread because you wanted your friend to cancel and can't articulate why. You catch your reflection and want to cry; not over how you look, but over how you feel inside. That's when you unravel. Agonize over scenarios that will never happen. Overa̶ll ▮▮▮ o▮n▮ that already played out. Scroll mind▮e̶sly through social media when you should b▮▮▮▮▮u▮▮▮t meet your friend at 8:00. It's already 8:15. You lie and text, *on my way*. You splash water on your face. Get your breathing under control. You're not going to be on time, but you will be there. You are going to be late. A̶gain. You are going to blame the traffic, not your anxiety. Again.

Currently listening to:
"That's What Friends Are For"
by Dionne Warwick

Track Forty-Three

Life is a mix of choices and chance.
A cross between best of luck
and best-laid plans.

Sometimes it feels like the cards
I've been dealt
were shuffled by the Devil himself.
I can read his tell.

Adam never needed to learn;
he had Eve up his sleeve.

I don't go to church anymore unless
someone is baptized, married, or dead;
but I still bless myself whenever
I am about to run a red
and keep the palm cross
tucked in my car above my head.

I let men with biblical names drag me
through Hell for the art it creates.
Have you seen my faith?
It seems to have been misplaced
somewhere beyond the saints, and
snakes, and apples, and gardens.

Forgive me, Father, or don't,
I'm not really looking for a pardon.

Currently listening to:
"Beautiful Ghosts" by Taylor Swift

Track Forty-Four

~~So much of me belongs to people who no longer breathe. It doesn't leave much for the ones still around me.~~

~~Graveyards are for your bones and my tears, for your name engraved and superimposed. Graveyards are for the mourning doves and old memories and new soil.~~

I'm usually the only person here, ~~shooing away the geese.~~
~~Why do lines wrap around the corners of funeral homes, but the cemeteries are always empty?~~

~~Where are the lines?~~

~~Where was the line when I could no longer conjure the sound of your voice?~~

~~Where was the line the first time I heard your laugh come out of someone else's throat?~~

~~Where was the line when they demolished our favorite spot?~~

~~Where was the line when your scent left the pillow or the day I realized I'd seen every single photo of us together and cried?~~

~~Where was the line on your birthday, or~~
~~my birthday, or that random~~

~~Wednesday when I needed you just~~
~~because?~~

~~Where are the lines?~~

The living ~~speak of normal~~
~~as if there is such a thing.~~
~~Even the mundane is insane~~
~~when you are bereaved.~~
~~I am starting to believe it's all a game;~~
~~that the ones who remain are only here~~
~~because we won a round~~
~~of musical graves.~~
~~We were still breathing~~
~~when the music stopped.~~

~~A cardinal lands,~~
~~the patron bird~~
~~of those who have passed.~~
~~The lines are gone,~~
~~but you,~~
 you ~~are~~ still ~~here.~~

Currently listening to:
"Bring My Flowers Now" by Tanya Tucker

Track Forty-Five

You have your headphones on with no music playing; you just want to pretend you can't hear what they're saying. You've adapted to your own mind. AS IN, even your heavy thoughts seem light. AS IN, your eye hardly twitches anymore. AS IN, you've adjusted to your sleep schedule. AS IN you don't sleep much at all but found the perfect under-eye concealer.

It's only when you're in a room filled with people not wired in such a way that you realize how close you are to short-circuiting. You are fried. Burned out. Praying for a factory reset you know won't come.

Life tripped you up then challenged you to keep up. Life continued to outpace your strides even after it saw you slumped over, gasping for air. Life kept moving forward even after you began lying to the people around you. AS IN, you didn't say your behavior was directly related to your reluctant metal coping. AS IN, you said that you were busy, not broken.

Currently listening to:
"Secrets" by Mary Lambert

Track Forty-Six

Biting my loose tongue
listening to Whitney in Houston,
I Wanna Dance with Somebody
who won't leave when the song is done.

I yearned to *Run to You*
when you flew away.
I yearned to *Run to You*
but my flight was delayed.

Will I always fall for the Drifters,
the Rolling Stones, and shape-shifters?
Won't somebody *Stand by Me*
for more than just one picture?

Room Full of Tears,
and all of them mine.
Room Full of Tears,
I needed a sign.

Riding shotgun in a *Fast Car*
with Tracy Chapman and her guitar.
Couldn't choose between the *Crossroads*
so I ran out of gas, never made it far.

Give Me One Reason
to glance in my rearview.
Give Me One Reason
to be near you.

Unobstructed skyline,
I reminisce when I hear Sublime,
about ocean fronts, dollar beers,
and the *Summertime*.

Love was *What I Got*
when I got you.
Indifference was *What I Got*
when we fell through.

Months go by,
trying to see the *Brightside*.
So I ~~run~~ t~~he sailo~~rs
and breathe in high tide.

All the Things I Have Done
weigh on my shoulders,
All the Things I Have Done
brought me my closure.

Sittin' on the Dock of the Bay,
contemplatin' the Otis-way.
Boats bob against weathered posts,
my broken heart still has good days.

I've Been Loving You Too Long
to remember much else.
I've Been Loving You Too Long,
I need to find myself.

Survived all Four Seasons
of your exit with no reasons.
When you miss me, *Tell It to the Rain.*
I found something new to believe in.

Oh, What a Night
it was when I let you go.
Oh, What a Night
it is to go on with the show.

Currently listening to:
"Good Thing" by Zedd and Kehlani

Track Forty-Seven

I've been using the energy I can muster
to force together apologies and promises
like a child frustrated that the puzzle
pieces don't fit, when they absolutely
look like they should.

I'm sorry I'm so tired;
   I promise I'll go to sleep early tonight.

I'm sorry I just want to lay around;
   I promise we'll go out tomorrow.

I'm sorry I don't want to have sex;
   I promise I'll want to in the morning.

I'm sorry the dirty clothes are piling up;
   I promise I'll do laundry this weekend.

I'm sorry if I
"seemed better" on Monday;
      I promise I'll be "better"
                        by Wednesday.

I'm sorry I'm not the person
you fell in love with;
   I promise we'll get back there.

I'm sorry you miss the person
I once was;
   I promise I miss that person too.

(That last one I actually mean.)

Currently listening to:
"It Had to Be You" by Ray Charles

Track Forty-Eight

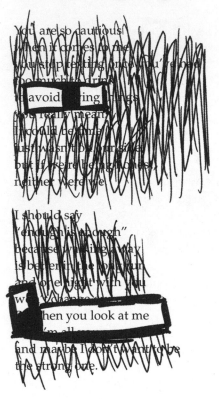

174

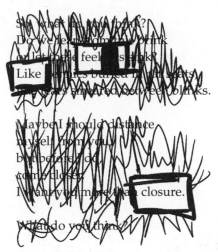

Currently listening to:
"No Parade" by Jordin Sparks

Track Forty-Nine

I joined the Mile Cry Club en route to
Portland, hovering 30,000 feet over
everything makes even the most chaotic
life look like nothing but a dazzling
mother-of-the-bride dress.

It's a false sense of freedom.

Momentarily, I'm a golden-winged
warbler, with crisis sonar warning me to
soar away before shit hits the fan.

But storm avoidance and crafty flight
patterns are just momentary
manufactured exhales.

And like that tiny bird,
it's always a round trip back home
to things I need to face
once the worst of it passes.

Currently listening to:
"Fidelity" by Regina Spektor

Track Fifty

Thunder rolls.
~~Bells begin to dance.~~
Pieces of  litter this coast.

~~Each time I'm here~~
~~I swear my heels seep into the sand a~~
~~little bit more.~~

This place is still trying *swallow*
whole.

I ~~tell you~~ returning feels like
~~visiting my own grave and you finally~~
~~understand why I only come back~~
~~on holidays and milestones, with~~
~~flowers in my hands.~~

~~If the tide has the right to ebb and flow,~~
~~to come and go, so do~~ I.

Currently listening to:
"Big Yellow Taxi" by Joni Mitchell

Track Fifty-One

You died, and I survived.

You died, and I became a person
you will never meet.

Someone you would not have
recognized on the street.

And that's what I can't shake.

You would have never known this
self, if incarnation, since I am certain I
am only this person because you left;
someone who would make you proud.

Death gives birth to advocates every
minute. Born again the day you died,
your spirit is alive in everything I do.

We will meet again one day, and you will
be the best, healthiest version of yourself
and I will be the best version of myself
and we will catch up over coffee and
buffalo fries and it will feel as though no
time has passed at all.

That helps me sleep at night.

Currently listening to:
"Change" by Christina Aguilera

Track Fifty-Two

I knew you were it when you laugh
made me smile and it took a while, but
we are here now; burning dinners,
swaying to the Spinners.

The way you sleep with one arm over
your head, how you hate that I keep my
socks on in bed. I'd choose us over and
over again.

The small moments,
the slowness, all of it.

Like how I know you chew ice
when you're nervous,
I am certain you are my person.

Our fairy tale
is in the details.

Currently listening to:
"I'll Call U Back" by Erykah Badu

Track Fifty-Three

You ~~gave me the~~ best gift. You left. You left and you didn't come back no matter how much I cried. No matter how much you cried. No matter ~~how many~~ times you got in your car only to turn around before arriving to our past. No matter how many times the wrong headlights in my driveway ~~made my stomach~~ sink. No matter how many times I screamed that you were killing me. No matter how much hearing that killed you. No matter how many times I warned you we were maki ng a mistake. No matter how many times you thought so too. No matter how many unsaid words floated between us in email drafts and half-dialed phone numbers. You gave me the best gift. You broke my heart. You left. And you stayed gone. I want to thank you for that.

Currently listening to:
"Sandcastles" by Beyoncé

Track Fifty-Four

our   hearts

shake

in

time together

Currently listening to:
"I Belong to You" by Brandi Carlile

Track fifty-five

~~You~~ ~~cellular reflection blinked when~~ ~~you didn't. You've been robotic for quite~~ ~~some time. Words tumble out of your~~ ~~throat and you don't recognize your~~ ~~own voice.~~

~~You liken yourself to~~ a
failed experiment

~~Given light eyes — but a heavy mind.~~
~~Given friends — but lonely.~~

~~For many years you were told you were~~
~~overreacting   lazy   sensitive.~~

~~You are none of those things.~~
~~You are learning the lessons of your life~~

~~in memory~~
~~then all you know.~~

~~Which made my notion of normalcy~~
~~seem~~ fleeting ~~space for you.~~
~~When you've become an adult~~
~~that waits for things to go wrong.~~
~~That searches for things to fix.~~
~~Which resulted in a wounded~~ heart
~~covered in bite marks.~~

Currently listening to:
"Bulletproof" by La Roux

Track Fifty-Six

It's finding the stamps and envelope but missing the energy to drive to the mailbox. It's craving a coffee, traveling fifteen minutes to get it, but then turning around because the place is packed with too many people. It's keeping your gaslight on because you just want to get home and can't imagine making another stop. It's messing up dinner, then crying because it's obviously the end of the world. It's being tired all day, then your head hits the pillow, and you're awake. It's wanting to make plans. It's wanting to return that text. It's wanting to call someone. It's wanting to be how everyone expects you to be. It's that word on the tip-of-your-tongue feeling, but you just can't find the words so you feel defective. And it's all of that happening in just one day.

Currently listening to:
"Again" by Janet Jackson

Track Fifty-Seven

Every time you tuck my hair behind my ear, or cradle my face between your palms, I think you want to tell me you are falling in love with me. Every time you look at me and your eyes become a little sad, I think you want to tell me you are falling in love with me. Every time you kiss my hand or forehead or knees, I think you want to tell me you are falling in love with me. Every time you stare at me until I look away, I think you want to tell me you are falling in love with me. Every time there is a stretch of silence that would make any other two people uncomfortable, I think you want to tell me you are falling in love with me.

Or maybe I have it backward.
Maybe I am the one
who wants to tell you.

Currently listening to:
"There's No Way" by Lauv
(featuring Julia Michaels)

Track Fifty-Eight

ache and grieve

kind

Currently listening to:
"The Sign" by Ace of Base

Track Fifty-Nine

~~We may walk the same earth,~~
~~but we inhabit very different~~ world
~~We all take in oxygen,~~
~~but the air tastes different~~
~~about tongues.~~
~~We are all just passing through~~
~~each other's world~~
~~as visitors, tourists.~~
~~We only see what is presented,~~
offer up.

~~Some people cannot fathom the notion~~
~~of not truly knowing anything~~
~~about a person.~~
Strangers ~~orbiting my world~~
~~think they know~~
~~what it's like to land,~~
~~stick down a flag, and live here.~~

~~What fools!~~

~~To think they can survive~~
~~away in my ecosystem,~~
when ~~I~~ often ~~find~~ myself lost
in ~~the uncharted~~ territory,
~~of my own existence.~~

~~What fools!~~

~~To think they are within reach~~
~~of the truth,~~
~~when they are~~ light years
~~from my reality.~~

Currently listening to:
"We're Going to Be Friends" by The White Stripes

Track Sixty

I've a̶l̶w̶a̶y̶s̶ ̶l̶i̶k̶e̶d̶ more prose than poetry, more open-ended than happy ending.

I read book acknowledgments first because I like to know who the author had in their heart when they wrote the book.

I respect people who order their coffee extra hot or with light ice because I think they know exactly what they want out of life. I find it sexy when a person knows how to parallel park. There might be nothing smoother.

I don't think socks have to match and that it's silly that so many spend so much of their limited time on earth folding them together, or searching for their matches, like socks could have a sole mate. I appreciate puns.

I am at a point in my life when I want more authenticity, less brand. More honesty, less beating perimeters of bushes to death.

You miss me?
Tell me.
You want me?
Tell me.

Because I am tired of moonlighting as
the person who's not in love with you.

You're hurting?
Tell me.
You're worried?
Tell me.

Because it's nice and human to have
these things in common.

Currently listening to:
"Let Me Go" by Alesso and Hailee Steinfeld
(featuring Florida Georgia Line)

Track Sixty-One

When you and I first met,
I was depressed and
you were underdressed,
but sitting across from you,
I swear I knew it then.

Now my fingers are running
through your hair.
Your hands, they feel like
coming home.
It's like they've always
belonged here.

Views of the Hudson River,
setting sun and French fries.
My favorite things to borrow
are you and time.

The City is twenty-two miles
past our breeze
but its lights feel warm,
within reach,
as if it could wash up on the beach.

Nothing, nothing
but hazel and blue—
the smell of your shampoo.
Nothing, nothing
but me and you—
so overdue.

Currently listening to:
"Here with Me" by The Killers

Track Sixty-Two

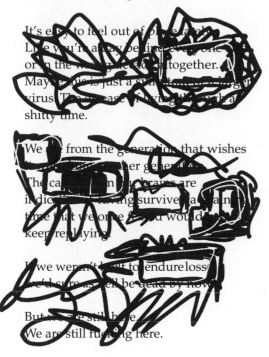

It's e___ to feel out of pl__e ___
Li_e y_u're al___y be___ ev___one _
or __ the w____g __ce__together.
May__ __is is just a s___tion c____ing _
virus. The __sease of living th___gh a
shitty time.

We ___ from the g_neration that wishes
_____ ___her gene_____.
The ca__ ____ in __ brains are
i_ dic_____ __ing survive_ a __a __ __
ti__ __at _e o__e __ _d would __
keep replaying.

I_ we weren't b___lt to endure loss,
__'d su_e __ __ll be dead by _ow.

But __ __e still h_re.
We are still fu___ng here.

Currently listening to:
"Rivers and Roads" by The Head and the Heart

Track Sixty-Three

I'm nothing but
a product
of my environment
and that's what you don't get.
My wit is a weapon I keep sharp.
I lock the doors behind
myself immediately,
fasten the wrought-iron bars
across my heart
I don't trust easy.
I'm a species endangered.
I look over my shoulder.
I don't speak to strangers,
I'm way too in tune with the danger.
If you manage to make it inside,
take what you want,
but leave me my life.

Currently listening to:
"Extraordinary Machine" by Fiona Apple

Track Sixty-four

He had to convince the pharmacist
that he disposed of his old amoxicillin
before she handed over the new script,
but the cashier didn't bat an eye
when he spent $75 at the liquor store.

Her driver's license
had to be scanned by the man
to buy over-the-counter pills,
but the cashier didn't think twice
when she spent $90 at the liquor store.

Currently listening to:
"Jenny from the Block" by Jennifer Lopez
(featuring Jadakiss and Styles P)

Track Sixty-Five

I loved ▮▮ u too much.

"Strangers" ▮▮ the wrong ▮ord for what
this is becau▮▮ ▮▮ch other on a
molecular level.

You ▮ew I had a ▮▮ ▮▮ ▮▮ n
▮ ▮ky nail and ▮▮ I consider▮▮
three-tined forks p▮▮ ▮▮ ▮y
foot twitched whenever I got tired.

I knew you only ▮ the ▮ling of Oreos
and took two hou▮ ▮▮ e a three-
sentence email and brushed your teeth
seven times a day.

You may be a "stranger" now, but your
mouth has c▮▮▮l every inch of my
body and I ▮ r▮ gnize your
deodorant o▮ ▮▮ ▮f me
at the bank ▮ ▮ea▮ ▮ ugh
rattle throug▮ ▮▮ ▮n
something supremely funny happens.

I lov▮ you ▮o much.

Being strangers isn't enough distance
for me. I can't unmeet you. Let's call this
w▮▮ ▮▮u're more of a ghost
th▮ a stranger.

I loved you too much.

Currently listening to:
"You're So Last Summer" by Taking Back Sunday

Track Sixty-Six

I haven't flipped the calendar since August / I just want to pause it / I got wrapped up trying to catch up from my time away / Barely caught my breath today / I was a bit disheveled but my mental state stayed level against my throbbing temple / It's perplexing / Because there's always a next thing that keeps me neglecting / What should matter more to me / Like my family and my REM cycle / It's easy to become unbridled / The world has gone crazy / Our vision is gone crazy / I need to stop and smell the daisies to ease my mind / I am worried about mankind / That we're going to run out of time / And soon / Maybe it's the full moon that's got me feeling unbalanced / I mean no malice / My brain is delicate and bruised / Not a bomb that needs to be defused.

Currently listening to:
"At the End" by Katherine Quintana

Track Sixty-Seven

Life will toss you things harder to
transform ▮▮▮▮▮s Sometimes life
will hand you things that will set your
hands on fire. And my world has been
on fire before. Limited visibility. Only
seeing the moment ▮▮▮▮ of me.

DO NOT ASK ME WHAT I AM DOING
NEXT WEEK. I DO NOT KNOW.

Don't light that match, I am covered in
gasoline, can't you smell it?

Heat rising from ▮▮▮▮▮ to my throat.
Spending weeks, months, inhaling ash
from the dysfunction, coughing from
the smoke.

Picking out funeral dresses, making sure
it's something I would never want to
wear again.

Taking sleeping pills, because if I woke
up after noon, there are fewer hours in the
day ▮▮ something terrible to happen.

Putting my phone on silent. Only check
it when I know I could handle bad
news.

Screaming.
Vomiting.
Praying.
So much praying.
Crying.
So much crying.

If water extinguishes most fires, tell me
why my tears singe my face. Tell me
why the streaks remain—burns upon
my cheeks. If what didn't kill me will
really make me stronger, tell me why I
still can't gather my strength to fight
back sometimes.

Currently listening to:
"Moves" by Big Sean

Track Sixty-Eight

Thought we'd have it
together by now. Figured out.
But we're still scrambling.
We still go on cold walks without a coat.
We still shut down, want to implode.
We still create space
so there's no room to be let down.

Yet, even at our most fucked up,
we were able to sleep.
So what the fuck is this?
Everything is so loud in this black hole
and voids aren't supposed to
make noise.
So what the fuck is this?

To avoid waking up somber,
I started going to bed sober.
Clear eyes and clarity
replaced disorientation and defeat.

How many bad days
need to add up to equal bad life?
The limit does not exist.
Even the days that you fall backward,
or spin in circles in the of advancing
forward, are made up of twenty-four
hours that turn into tomorrow.

And as long as there is tomorrow,
there is hope.

Currently listening to:
"Dedicated to the One I Love"
by The Mamas and the Papas

Track Sixty-Nine

I wish I could

convince

You forgive

t o

The dark and

create a home in hope this year

Currently listening to:
"You're My Best Friend" by Queen

Track Seventy

I remember w   us,
                                     before the
                        cracked

promises   knew

                                    too.

Currently listening to:
"Ocean Avenue" by Yellowcard

Track Seventy-One

Your ▮▮ are ▮▮▮▮▮▮▮▮
▮▮▮▮▮ imagined them to be,
as if they have never
been kissed with urgency.

(Until now.)

Thi▮ ▮ving, this "you and me,"
t▮ ▮m▮ ▮hat i▮▮▮▮
th▮ ▮v▮ ▮ev▮▮ dream ▮▮,
because I've never been one
t▮ ▮▮▮▮ ▮▮▮▮
S▮ I hope, you ▮e somewhere
I ▮ stay ▮▮▮ ast one more day.

Or for always.

(Either wa▮▮▮
        I love you.

Currently listening to:
"Enchanted" by Taylor Swift

Track Seventy-Two

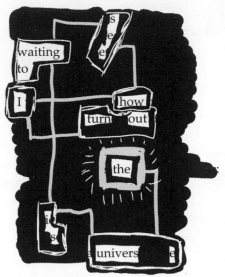

Currently listening to:
"I'm Still Standing" by Elton John

Track Seventy-Three

Once, the shower heat escaped the bathroom and I just wished it would burn the house down. That was where I was at. I had never been so fucking tired before. I was falling apart more that I wasn't. I wrote the saddest poem of my life sitting on a sunny beach in the Hamptons. I hadn't showered for three days and was taking shit to sleep when I got the call about my first book deal. I got into an argument with you in the middle of Broome Street because "was always sad" and "my sadness" had begun to seep into other things, like your life.

I wanted to scream back that if you had gone through what I had, you would be worse off. A hermit. Maybe dead. Your peripheral pain was just a graze compared to my wounds. But I was too defeated to care about winning a drunken fight in SoHo. So I hailed a cab.

I wanted to tell you that night on Broome Street that I didn't choose agony. It chose me. I chose to survive though. I chose to welcome happiness with open arms when it would momentarily shine through, like light through curtains. I chose coping skills and scary conversations and recovery.

Currently listening to:
"Be Careful" by Cardi B

Track Seventy-Four

If I am being honest, I knew you weren't
the one a few weeks in when you bit
directly into a string cheese. I knew, and
yet, I allowed you to continue to go
against my grain and take up space for
410 days.

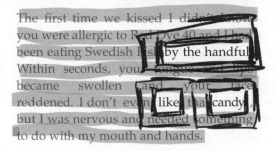

The first time we kissed I didn't know
you were allergic to Red Dye 40 and I had
been eating Swedish fish by the handful.
Within seconds, your tongue and lips
became swollen and your face
reddened. I don't even like that candy,
but I was nervous and needed something
to do with my mouth and hands.

We weren't right for a bunch of other,
more fatal, serious, non-hypoallergenic
reasons too, but sometimes it's that
simple.

String-cheese-simple.

Everyone used to say how great we looked together. As if looking great and fitting together were one and the same. When I finally left, my friends asked me why.

I told them that every time I was driving us somewhere, you would alert me whenever someone was in my blind spot. You would grab the oh-shit handle, your knuckles would turn white, and scream that someone was in the next lane. Even when I had no intention of switching lanes.

I knew that if you couldn't trust me to get us somewhere safely a mile up the road, you were never going to trust me with the bigger stuff. And anyone who is with me long enough will no doubt see the bigger stuff. Now I am in your blind spot — now you will never see me again.

Currently listening to:
"Hold On" by Alabama Shakes

Track Seventy-Five

I used to think moths were butterflies
that had grown old.

I used to think birds sang because they
were happy.

Used to think chemo was a cure.

Used to think rain came from holes in
clouds.

That the moon could only be seen at
night.

That *I love you* meant *I'll stay.*

Straw homes are built from
misconceptions. We adapt to the drafts
that whistle through these false truths
until we see them for what they really
are, wolves dressed in delusion's clothing.

I used to think only textbook alcoholics
should stop drinking.

I used to think ~~rest was~~ the natural state
of all objects ~~that everything~~ that
moves will ~~eventually~~ come to a stop.

But the makeup of my mind runs on
and on and on, even when I plead for a
pause.

I used to think ~~a lot of things~~
until I began ~~to live and learn~~ and know.

Currently listening to:
"Burning House" by Cam

Track Seventy-Six

▮ the time you text me your regret,
I▮m already eastbound and down.
▮ne▮er thought I would leave.
Well, neither did I.

I always bought the ticket but ne▮er ▮ot
o▮ ▮he plane. I always imagine ▮moving▮
▮on ▮ut my feet remained entangled
with our ruins.

I always kept the million reasons I had
to walk away packed haphazardly in
my go-bag. Nothing momentous
happened the d▮y I actually ▮eft. There
was no big fight, no ▮r▮nd reveal.

There was just me and the echo of my
f▮▮▮▮▮▮▮▮▮▮▮ound ▮ house
that didn't feel like home anymore.

Currently listening to:
"Chasing the Sun" by Chris Rockwell
(featuring Alix Gagliastro)

Track Seventy-Seven

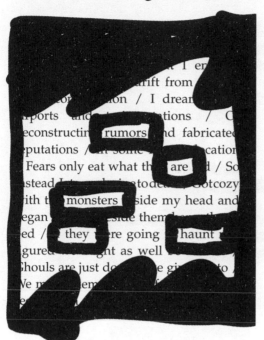

Currently listening to:
"Take It on the Run" by REO Speedwagon

Track Seventy-Eight

In the process of fighting

over and over and over again,

the monster

turn

I washed

in to

the prey

Currently listening to:
"Started From the Bottom" by Drake

Track Seventy-Nine

Now that your lips have been on mine
I wonder how they will feel
other places.
If this is what a fall from grace is,
God, let me keep falling—
because I'm all in.

People who see me say I glow,
like I know something they don't.
I want to remember it all,
so I could miss it if it goes.

God, let me keep falling—
because I'm all in.
All in.

I'll write about us
until the words no longer fit.

I am all in.
All in.

Currently listening to:
"MIDDLE CHILD" by J. Cole

Track Eighty

We are all m
o water an
Both are necessary
Neither is poison.

You had to show up for others
for a long time.
Be a safe harbor. A therapist
A mediator.
An encyclopedia. A lighthouse.

Aftermaths became cozy.

You let others cry, vent, scream
All the while, your pain was rising to
the surface and there'd be this
screeching-teapot ringing in your ear.
You would pull into a CVS parking lot
or run the shower and cry in secret.
You'd scream internally or into a pillow.

Then answer the phone like you hadn't
been up for two days straight.
Not because others expected you to
never have your own breakdowns.
But because you sincerely thought if
they saw you crumble
they would crumble even more and you
didn't want that for them.

212

You wanted them to get better.
So, you stayed quiet.
And let it destroy you
from the inside, out.

Let those years serve as a learning
moment. You'll never stop showing up
for people, but you'll never put yourself
through it that way again.

We are in repair, never beyond repair.
We are healing, never healed.

Currently listening to:
"What Do You Hear in These Sounds" by Dar Williams

213

Track Eighty-One

When you're *other*, you will lose time.
You will be less reason, more rhyme.
You will self-medicate your mind
to ease the havoc and clutter.
You'll sleep alone in the gutter.
Your light will crackle the sky,
you'll disrupt like thunder.
When you're *other*.

When your eyes see the world
in an odd small way,
opinions of the majority will sway,
but hardly land in your favor.

When you can make beauty
out of your pain,
you'll be an outsider until you decay,
then they'll call you a trailblazer.

When you're *other*,
it is easy to feel alone,
though you feel you're best
on your own.
It's easy to find yourself lost,
when your faith and trust
have been crossed.
Easy to question your sanity
when your art stems from tragedy.

When you're *other*,
the world will seem overcrowded
by perceptions that are clouded.
You will yearn for a safe haven,
a forest of creation.
Then, a place will call out to you:
"You are *other*, run for cover."

214

It's a place
to breathe new breath.
To gather strength.
To reach new lengths.
To shut your eyes
and count to ten.

It's a place to dance with
the skeletons in your closet,
take turns waltzing with
the reasons that caused this.
As they stretch their bones
and regrow their flesh,
you will thank them for
creating this mess.

Because here, you will find your peace
in who you are, in how you think,
in how you see things differently.
And at the top of your lungs
you will sing:

"I am *other*, one of a kind.
There are no flaws in my design.
You cannot keep me confined.
Stars seek me out to sleep over.
Even in dark, I find color.
I will raise up those who suffer.
I search for rain, not for level.
My light will adorn the sky,
I'll erupt like thunder.
I am *other*."

Currently listening to:
"To Hell & Back" by Maren Morris

Track Eighty-Two

Ice patches float on top of the lake like lily pads do in the muggy months. The wind has not been able to budge the water for weeks and is making up for lost time.

Snow dusts the surrounding pines, reminding me of the small artificial trees my great-grandmother used to meticulously place within her miniature Christmas village. It's the type of beautiful that I know my cracked screen won't replicate, so when I show people later, they won't understand why I was so captivated.

I don't feel this serene often. My changing seasons was not as graceful as this; no one would have stopped and appreciated what they saw. It was more akin to being eaten alive by fire ants. Dragonflies would often land on my chest or elbows during this time, an omen of things to come.

There is no growth without breakage, nothing to salvage without a wreckage to scour. I survived wounds my therapist warned could prove fatal, and today I got to see the most beautiful lake begin to thaw back to life right before my eyes.

Currently listening to:
"Feeling Good" by Nina Simone

Track Eighty-Three

Currently listening to:
"If I Could" by Regina Belle

Track Eighty-Four

The past is not something we can simply place down on a coffee table or leave behind at an airport. The past is a part of us; sometimes for better, mostly for worse, but a part of us nonetheless. To think we can simply "let go" of the past is just as silly as thinking we need to offer up who we are today as sacrificial lambs in order to become who we will be tomorrow. It's all so tethered and rooted that it feels fluid.

We cannot ▮▮▮▮▮▮▮▮▮▮▮▮▮ay. We can't forget, not completely. But we can accept some things will always look more picturesque—seem more serene— from a safe distance, from a faint recollection, and we can move forward. It is imperative that we always move forward.

Currently listening to:
"How Far We've Come" by Matchbox Twenty

Track Eighty-Five

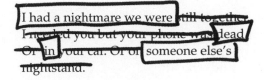

I had a nightmare we were still together.
I needed you but your phone was dead.
Or in your car. Or on someone else's
nightstand.

~~I WOKE UP TIRED~~

~~Even in a dreamworld,~~
~~your bullshit exhausts me.~~
~~Even in a dreamworld,~~
~~you can't show up for me.~~
~~Even in a dreamworld,~~
~~we would never work out.~~

~~The nightmare is no longer~~
~~perpetual, though.~~

~~I GET TO WAKE UP~~

Currently listening to:
"Nightmare" by Halsey

Track Eighty-Six

We live in a world where guns and the
flu are killing children whose older
siblings are already dying off from
heroin and fentanyl and other drugs
their parents explain away to them by
saying, "She took too much medicine
and lives in Heaven now."

We live in a world where when I ask a
ten-year-old what he wants to be when
he grows up, instead of saying an
astronaut or firefighter or president, he
just replies, "Here, I still want to be here
when I grow up."

And I know here means *alive*.

And I wonder when understanding the
fragility of one's mortality was lumped
in with teaching fractions and cursive
and the state capitals.

And with two decades between us,
looking in his eyes and they look older
than mine. My heart breaks at his
statement as tears roll down my face
but he doesn't ask me why, because
there are two decades between us, and
he is still only a child.

Currently listening to:
"What I Never Knew I Always Wanted"
by Carrie Underwood

Track Eighty-Seven

Be like water. Fill every space like it was made just for you, like you belong there. Yes, there's a risk you'll pour over and soak whatever is near, but water doesn't worry about what it wets; it just flows or falls. Water doesn't apologize, and most days it just dries, melts, or freezes like it was never there. But sometimes it leaves a mark behind—it all depends on what it touches. Don't be afraid to leave behind a mark. Be like water.

Currently listening to:
"Little Wonders" by Rob Thomas

Track Eighty-Eight

I spend so much time trying to outrun who I once was that I sometimes throw away the notion that there are pieces of me worth salvaging.

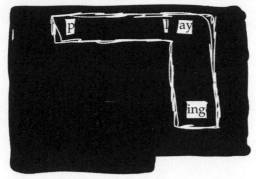

The part of me that decorates three trees and remains enchanted by Christmas lights. The part of me that acts surprised whenever my nephew finds me in a game of hide and seek.

These parts—not my job or my weight or
my clothes or the size of my house—are
the parts of me that if I were to lose, I'd
lose touch with myself and begin

f
l
o
a
t
i
n
g

lost   in   space.

Currently listening to:
"When My Train Pulls In (Acoustic)"
by Gary Clark Jr.

Track Eighty-Nine

The lig blink ber,
th tre down.
An over
d own.

Things haven't been the same
since the hurricane came.
It's been two years since I've
stepped into the arcade.
At one poi i y life,
I used to t e every day.

The Exx is e,
the paint ipped off the chapel.
Catch in my lungs,
never enough oxygen in a time capsule.

The lights blink amber,
the street signs .
Another summ over
for this seaside

Currently listening to:
"I Miss You" by Blink 182

Track Ninety

You try to count up how many versions
of yourself were sacrificed in exchange
for the person you are today.
You lose track after running out of
fingers and toes and those
tiny tiles on the bathroom wall.
Stop trying to reverse-engineer
what brought you here.
The iterations do not matter.
What matters is that you shed skin
trusting that you'd never reach bone.
What matters is you cried tears,
knowing that you wouldn't drown.
What matters is you believed others
when they told you that you mattered.

What matters is you
kept believing
you mattered too.

Currently listening to:
"Carry On" by fun.

Track Ninety-One

The stillne   inside of me is   ne,
leaked th
That's   ppens when   weight
of the world leaves your sho
enters your head.

I no longer can sit silent with myself.
I pace. Race. Twitch. Itch.
Did I leave th   on?
Did I blow   that   ndle?
Did I lock th
Better go back and check.

The   will always   things to fix,
to o
The worries are infinite;
the days are finite.

This life.
This world as you know it right now,
filled with the people you love,
will be gone one day.

So, when you feel the sadn   linge
remember not every guidin
       w bright.
There   a lesson found
       ur days,
even hidden in the
worst ones of your life.

Carry on, carry on.

Currently listening to:
"On + Off" by Maggie Rogers

Track Ninety-Two

I need you

to live
a long time

and

always

rest
And

begin

Currently listening to:
"Thankful" by Kelly Clarkson

National Suicide Prevention Lifeline

1-800-273-8255

Connect with Alicia

Instagram: @thealiciacook

Twitter: @the_alicia_cook

www.thealiciacook.com

Additional Notes: SIDE A

Track 6: Originally published in *Nervous Ghost Press*

Track 15: Originally published in *[Dis]Connected II: Poems & Stories of Connection and Otherwise*

Tracks 24 + 33: The original versions were created in songwriting sessions with Carly Moffa

Tracks 61 + 79: The original versions were created in a songwriting session with Highland Kites

Track 81: Originally published in *[Dis]Connected II: Poems & Stories of Connection and Otherwise*

Track 83: Inspired by a poetry writing prompt created by Kat Savage and J.R.Rogue

Track 91: Two lines were inspired by a poetry writing prompt created by Amanda Torroni

Andrews McMeel Publishing
a division of Andrews McMeel Universal
1130 Walnut Street, Kansas City, Missouri 64106

www.andrewsmcmeel.com

23 24 25 26 27 VEP 11 10 9 8 7

ISBN: 978-1-5248-6052-3

Library of Congress Control Number: 2020941797

Illustration by Katie Curcio

Editor: Patty Rice
Art Director/Designer: Julie Barnes
Production Editor: Margaret Daniels
Production Manager: Cliff Koehler

ATTENTION: SCHOOLS AND BUSINESSES
Andrews McMeel books are available at quantity discounts with bulk purchase for educational, business, or sales promotional use. For information, please e-mail the Andrews McMeel Publishing Special Sales Department: sales@amuniversal.com.